# COLLEGE WRITING

# COLLEGE WRITING
*Entertaining Writing on Everyday Topics*

### By Tom Friedrich

*Plattsburgh State University*

cognella®
SAN DIEGO

Bassim Hamadeh, CEO and Publisher
John Remington, Executive Editor
Gem Rabanera, Project Editor
Alia Bales, Production Editor
Emely Villavicencio, Senior Graphic Designer
Trey Soto, Licensing Coordinator
Natalie Piccotti, Director of Marketing
Kassie Graves, Vice President of Editorial
Jamie Giganti, Director of Academic Publishing

Cover image:
Copyright © 2018 iStockphoto LP/maaram.
Copyright © 2018 iStockphoto LP/bigacis.
Copyright © 2018 iStockphoto LP/pepifoto.

Printed in the United States of America.

3970 Sorrento Valley Blvd., Ste. 500, San Diego, CA 92121

# CONTENTS

CHAPTER 4

Being a Community Member 73

CHAPTER 5

Being a Networked User 111

# PREFACE
## On Being Epicurean

Making academic writing reveal and enrich your most valued interests is a calculated risk to avoid cheap thrills and instead pursue rich pleasures. It's also part of a life well lived. In this preface, I describe the idea of a good life as the pursuit of profound pleasures, or being Epicurean. I introduce this pursuit by means of a personal anecdote, a brief description of what Epicureanism means, and a snack metaphor that illustrates why profound pleasures are better than cheap ones: because they're transformative.

## Meeting an Epicurean: A Trip to a Bar

In spring 1997, I visited my friend Denise for a weekend in her hometown, Sarasota, Florida. Seeing Denise was the best part of being there, of course, but the weather marked a nice break from springtime in Boston, where I lived at the time. Denise had also whetted my appetite for learning what made Florida, well, Florida, by describing features of the popular culture for me. Of course, there was Disney, but was there more? Denise said we had to visit an Irish bar she was fond of, and I was good to go. At first I did not see what made it special; I should not have been expecting a nineteenth-century establishment with gold lettering, engravings, and darkly stained wood creating a cavernous, hearth-like feel, but I was. In a strip mall—like pretty much everything in Sarasota—this was not that kind of pub, at least not on the face of it. Anyway, we went in and ordered whiskeys, and as I could immediately see, this place was special for the people—and the relationships Denise had built here. She knew everyone, it seemed, so well that she didn't even need to talk to them—a wave or a smile was just enough. There was one person she introduced me to, though: Jerry.

I can barely remember this man's appearance, but he was a middle-aged Irishman. He had had a drink or two. He was also incredibly sincere, open to meeting me in a way I hope I will learn to be to others before I die. I asked him about himself, how he got to Sarasota, and other things. His answers don't stay in my memory except for a summary comment he made: "I'm in heaven."

Now, I looked around this room, the fact that it was a bar—a bar in a strip mall, in a state living under the specter of Mickey Mouse—and his statement made little sense to me. How could this be heaven for anyone?

Jerry's statement has never left me, though. Rather, I've come to appreciate it by considering the Buddhist idea that life is suffering. So easily seduced by French fries and the desire for revenge, we know distracting cravings never end. Despite it all, there are things we do we know we love—and, rarer still, the moments when we immerse or lose ourselves in them. When I think of Jerry now, I think that he meant something like this—he was a bar saint, a man who embraced without flinching what he loved the most. He was, in a word, an Epicurean.

## What Does It Mean to Be an Epicurean?

To be an Epicurean means to make life an unending journey for what is most desirable. This does not mean to "do whatcha like"; instead, it means to embrace that reality is dynamic, so the best you can do is spend your time determining what is the greatest of goods and seeking it out. To point to one categorization I have found helpful, Roland Barthes (1975) distinguishes between the perceptions of "pleasure" and "bliss." On the one hand, there is "pleasure," the experience of a thing you know you like—such as a run-of-the-mill glazed donut—that satisfies your desires without transforming them. "Bliss," on the other hand, is the experience of a thing you don't know you like in advance—like a cheddar-and-bacon cupcake with a salted maple buttercream frosting for dessert—that, by satisfying your desires in the end, transforms them. Being an Epicurean doesn't mean pursuing "bliss" exclusively, but it definitely calls for much more than eating a bunch of average glazed donuts.

I like how Stephen Greenblatt describes being an Epicurean in *The Swerve* (2012). He quotes an excerpt from the core text guiding this classical philosophy, Lucretius's *On the Nature of Things*:

> It is comforting … to witness mighty clashes of warriors embattled on the plains, when you have no share of the danger. But nothing is more blissful than to occupy the heights effectively fortified by the teaching of the wise, tranquil sanctuaries from which you can look down upon others and see them wandering everywhere in their random search for the way of life, competing for intellectual eminence, disputing about rank, and striving night and day with prodigious effort to scale the summit of wealth and to secure power. (196)

This passage distinguishes between the "comforting," where "you" are a passive observer and the "blissful," where "you" are an active participant. In "occupy[ing] the heights," we are in cheddar-and-bacon cupcake country. It is a matter of seeing the world for what it is, avoiding pain-avoiding or pleasure-embracing "delusions" by, instead, accepting that reality—and humans as a part of it—is nothing more than, as Greenblatt puts it, "atoms" that "swerve." From an Epicurean perspective, this is a source of strength and hope. Why? To "occupy the heights," one must be committed to the idea that to know something, to perceive the truth, demands beginning with the conviction that I have stereotypes that keep me from perceiving what is actually there. I need to confess that I am not the center of the universe to see the divine.

## It's Time to Take a Bite: Academic Writing as an Epicurean, Entertaining Act

Moving beyond old thinking by challenging everyday stereotypes (such as what a good cupcake ought to taste like) is not just an Epicurean approach to life; it also describes what writing-to-learn can provide when it is embraced as the pleasure-seeking opportunity to "occupy the heights." Writing-to-learn means what it sounds like: not "just writing," but writing to come to know things. This writing isn't a test of what you already know. Rather, when you write-to-learn, you are on a path that you are ready to follow and may surprise you. You are a part of a dynamic world of which you are not the center. To use academic writing to make meaningful discoveries, then, you have to go on a journey. As far as this book is concerned, that journey involves using language to refine your worldview by investigating everyday life—topics such as being a student, a community member, and a digital tool user.

Every point about writing made hereafter leads back to a general point about life itself: a life lived well can be a decentering, Epicurean pursuit of pleasure. It is a difficult path because pleasure can never be achieved as a solid, bankable state. Does it take being strategic? Yes. Does it take being a good person? Yes. But both of those, as drivers—be reasonable to live well, be good to live well—seem hard to manage. Much easier, it seems to me, is the face of pleasure, like Jerry in the Florida bar.

Are you ready to "occupy the heights?" If to answer yes sounds audacious, let me close on this point: I believe that there are many divine encounters in this world and that they typically come in unexpected places, such as a cupcake that, based on stereotypes about what constitutes a good one, should not taste good but surprisingly tastes fantastically so. A salty and sweet cupcake? Oh, yes, my friend. Just start thinking salted caramel, and you will be on the way. But, as Martin Picard tells Anthony Bourdain in *Parts Unknown*, beaver tastes like beaver. In other words, there is no substitute for eating that cheddar-and-bacon cupcake.

It's time to take a bite.

# INTRODUCTION

I n this book, I argue that the best way to learn to do academic writing is by using it to learn more about topics that interest you. I don't say that lightly, as if "interest" were as easy to come by as a Chicken McNugget™. Instead, I embrace the idea that desire is difficult, that we generally are trying to figure out what we really want most of the time. Passing fancies are everywhere; lasting loves are what we want, so the trick is being able to discern between the two and choose the latter. That requires refining your judgment, and doing academic writing on a topic that interests you can help you improve at.

Can doing academic writing really help you to "occupy the heights?" Let me answer this question by providing an overview of this book's contents.

## An Overview of This Book's Chapters

Academic writing and reading can be experiences of pursuing bliss, and my aim in this book is to show you how. In Chapter 1, I begin by using my own history as a student writer to show how I came to believe self-respecting students ought to insist on experiencing academic writing as an entertaining activity. Then, I define the act of entertaining as involving two halves: play and performance. What is play? Play is, to me, a relationship with an object—like a basketball, a book, or even an idea—you find so meaningful it changes you somehow. A performance is a statement of your perspective on an object for an audience. There is no doubt in my mind that many student writers experience their performances as meaningless. What I am convinced of, however, is that when students have playful relationships with what they're writing on, those meaningless performances come to an end. So, what do these playful performances look like? I provide examples here, building toward an analysis of classical rhetoric that demonstrates I am not alone in celebrating the power of entertaining writing.

Chapter 2 argues academic "reading-to-write" can be a playful performance, too. Motivated reading-to-write, a concept I borrow from composition researcher Stuart Greene, is a different animal from "just reading." Reading-to-write requires approaching a text with a plan, using—or, as

Greene (1991) puts it, "mining"—a text to realize a goal as an author. When mining a text, a reader strategically pushes past her or his prejudices by making

> informed guesses about how to use the ideas or discourse features of a given text in light of his or her goals as a writer. Such an "excavation" can be a selfish endeavor for it serves the individual in his or her search for riches. But in excavating knowledge a developing author uses the object of inquiry to make a contribution to the community that shapes and constrains what is said and how it is communicated.

I agree with Greene's idea of textual mining, which, like entertaining writing, serves two masters: the writer and the reader. Like entertaining writing, entertaining reading-to-write has a twofold quality: like play and performance, it asks readers to first suspect and later decide what a text's argument is. It's a game of hunches and guesses getting confirmed and challenged, one you keep going on until you can't get any more confident that you've arrived. You keep asking "Is that it?" until you get as close to occupying the heights as you can. I finish by describing four reading-to-write strategies you may use in researching an everyday topic: outlining, summarizing, searching for phenomenological themes, or writing a Ketner card. (Curious? Read on.)

Because entertaining writing starts with an everyday topic, each of the final three chapters of the book is organized around a familiar role: being a student (Chapter 3), a community member (Chapter 4), and a networked digital tool user (Chapter 5). You have ideas about these familiar roles you can use in reading and writing to investigate and challenge. Each of these final chapters contains two parts:

**Role**: First, I introduce a role (e.g., being a student), grounding it in literature on the topic and autobiography. Whereas topic selection is a straightforward matter in Chapter 5, in Chapters 3 and 4—where it is not—I provide a number of strategies for arriving at one you find persuasive, arresting, *entertaining*.

**Genres**: Then, I present a sequence of two genres you can use to write-to-learn on the chapter's role. For each genre, I describe its characteristics, provide and analyze a student model of the genre-in-action, and offer prewriting and drafting strategies designed to help you do entertaining writing on your topic.

I don't intend for you to read any of these last three chapters in a single sitting. They are assignment sequences. I suggest reading the first third of the chapter to get familiar with the topic on one day; the second for one major assignment; and the third only after you've completed the first piece.

I'd like to make two other comments about this book. Does it emphasize revision? Yes, it does, particularly in Chapter 4, where it describes a revision task you can pair with any other genre described in Chapters 3 through 5. Also, there are two things this book does not include: readings or error descriptions and exercises. Yes, I refer to readings on each topic; where I could select open-access texts, I have. As a teacher, though, I pair other resources with this one, and I assume your teacher will do the same.

## "Give It Now": Conclusion

I don't give this overview of the book lightly. How did we get here from cupcakes? You might say, "I like cupcakes." *But do you like*, I might say in response, *really weird ones*? If you want to know, you need to take a chance. You do take a chance. Epicurean, entertaining writing means taking chances with language, and in my view, that's what writing needs to be. As I write this sentence, I sit in my basement, revising the book you hold in your hands. It's an exciting, yet vexing, situation to be in. I don't know how well it's going to work. I don't know if I'll ever be happy with it. All I know is that I believe in the book's idea, and I can seize this moment and try to write it as best I can. I think of the other things I could do today, and this one—no matter what I do—will not go away. So, I tell myself, sit down and—as Annie Dillard (2013) writes—"spend it all, shoot it, play it, lose it, all, right away, every time. Do not hoard what seems good for a later place in the book or for another book; give it, give it all, give it now" (78).

That's what it means to write to "occupy the heights." So do it, now, if you value your life.

## CHAPTER 1

# DON'T WASTE YOUR TIME, PART I

## (Or Writing as Entertainment)

In this chapter, I argue that academic writing can be an entertaining act by turning to my own experience of being a college writer as well as to sources ranging from a Trader Joe's bag to a Roman rhetorician named Quintilian. I use this review to conclude with the claim that the choice to write-to-learn is yours alone. Useful strategies at your disposal and a changing world, the study of which thereby yields new insights, make that a risk worth taking. It's a choice you'll want to make, as resisting it means wasting your time— learning nothing new—and embracing it puts you on a path to becoming a more purposeful, complete writer and person.

## No More Fortresses: How I Learned to Do Entertaining Academic Writing

It is easy to waste time in school. It is a kind of default stance to certain parts of the curriculum, such as the first-year writing class that is required at most U.S. colleges. I can recall the writing course I was required to take at St. Olaf College. I was excited about the subject matter, which was the French Revolution. A history major, this section had seemed it might appeal to me for obvious reasons. I took that class twenty-five years ago, so my memory is sketchy, but what I recall is that I felt inconsequential just about all of the time in that room. A lot of that may have been the B's I kept getting, which made me feel "good enough" but nothing else. I remember one woman, Amy, who had been in the course. She was quiet but cool, a short platinum blond with a pageboy haircut from New York City who got A's on everything she turned in. She had a subversive quality to her, yet I told myself she could afford to be this way because she mattered to our teacher. I felt I did not have the same freedom. I had to follow orders, and I was good at doing that.

I can't remember anything I wrote in that class, and although that may just be those twenty-five years talking, I can't help but think that how I wrote because I felt irrelevant is part of the reason why. I had been trying to say something passable about *The Great Cat Massacre* or *The Return of Martin Guerre*—about which I remember nothing but that in *Martin Guerre*, his whole village was apparently present when he first got into bed with his bride. That might have been an interesting topic, but I didn't want my professor to know me from my writing. Apparently, this professor actually flew home to his house in New Jersey every weekend, which to me was short for "There is nothing interesting here, including your ideas." I wanted to please him, to get the best grade I could—to have no impactful relationship on either side—and walk out psychologically intact and unchanged. I wanted points, not to be a different person.

I have very different memories of a course in creative writing that I took in my sophomore year. This course I had chosen to take, but I had had a sense of purpose with my composition course, too. A lot of what made this course memorable was that my teacher, Stephen Polansky, made it obvious that he taught with integrity and expected the same of us. Ironically, he said that while he required that we write poems, he refused to do so himself. Somehow, this brazen statement about his own limits gave him a contour, made him body and soul to me in ways his colleague could never be. I suppose what it comes down to, for me, is a couple of moments. I can see myself turning in a poem on the Dresden bombing during World War II.

I chose this topic because my relatives were from a village near there; I had visited them once, and it seemed page worthy. No one liked this lifeless poem, and the message I took away was that I had to write what I knew. So, that is what I did next: I wrote a poem about getting a cheeseburger in my hometown. It was about a Wendy's, a fact I left out because that might have made this place seem like any other—which it was not to me. I have always loved detail, interacting with objects as if they were living things, my cohabitants on earth, and that place had a memorable cash register—one where the coins traveled down a slide into a dish near the customer's hand. Unlike the restaurant's name, I put that coin slide I loved into my poem. I remember attending class soon after turning that poem in, at a meeting where Polansky shared my poem with the class in a workshop. This poem got better reviews. That moment marked me, let me know I could write with integrity in a class. Only with time did I come to see, though, how that class had given me even more: a life, a place at the table, something to say in a field of study, English.

As time went by, I maintained very unhelpful ideas about the differences between what James Britton (1975) calls "transactional" and "expressive" writing (93). I created expressive texts for people; I created transactional ones for no one. In other words, I maintained a sense that a story or poem was written as a relationship between the writer and his audience, whereas transactional ones were tests to be passed—the textual equivalent of a fortress that could be defended against attacks that it was uninformed. Being unreadable was fine—but uninformed was unacceptable, so mangled, stringy sentences pockmarked with citations, advancing as few controversial claims as possible, became my hallmark.

I continued to see writing this way until I had professors in graduate school who told me my transactional fortresses were horrible. Two people stand out. There was Arthur Weitzman, my Jane Austen professor, commenting on my draft of a paper on critics' reviews of director Ang Lee's cinematic adaptation of *Sense and Sensibility*. Sitting together in his office, my professor went through the first couple of pages with me, and he concerned himself with the quality of my argument and style. Regarding the former, Weitzman pointed out how more negative reviews were not necessarily better. I understood that, of course, but it drew my attention to how I had judged critics' comments: the higher the status of the publication a review came in, the more likely I was to consider it incisive. He went on. He drew attention to my verb choices, in particular my use of "manifest," which I saw as a spicy synonym for the verb "to make." No, he said. That is not what it means. If you mean "make," say "make." As with my logic regarding the reviews' quality, I had deferred to status—to words that appeared to carry authority. No. It was not working; what I had written was not good enough. Weitzman made me go home and make something readable and honest. So I did. What I remember most is spending a weekend with a printed-off copy of my draft and a pencil, scratching out lines and sections, filling in margins, working to arrive at a paper for a person. And I remember that when I turned it in and Weitzman mentioned he had seen a call for papers on Austen film adaptations, I actually thought about submitting mine.

When I wrote for Weitzman, I wrote transactional writing to be read, but it took me an experience soon after to see just why this mattered as much as it did. I was in a writing methods course for preservice teachers with Bonnie Sunstein. For this course, Sunstein assigned composition research monographs, whole books focused on the practices of particular student writers and writing teachers, among them Thomas Newkirk's *The Performance of Self in Student Writing* (1997). This is not what the late, great writing researcher George Hillocks (1986) might call a "natural process" book, one that vacates the teacher from the workshop, leaving students to turn whatever informal writing they found most meaningful into formal projects. Instead, Newkirk argues that teachers should frame student writing as a romantic activity. Newkirk does not say this because he believes an individual student can write to discover the absolute, unchanging essence of something. He knows the world we experience is always changing, anyway. Instead, Newkirk recommends teachers pitch transactional writing as a romantic activity to give students room to create more balanced texts—audience-oriented works that, nevertheless, taste of student writers' purposes. This valuing of purpose in Newkirk resonated with me. He gave me an axiom: the argument can be the writer's heart in a paper. Of course, there are many purposeless essays written every day—I have written many, not seeing another way. Of course, there are teachers who also say heart-killing things like this: "everything that could be argued, has been"; "really, the position you take is irrelevant; what matters is the quality of your argument, if it's a topic viewed by certain communities as important, if your evidence is compelling." As common as purposeless papers are, I knew they were not the only kind—I had Weitzman to thank for that. I knew transactional and expressive writing were different things, but thanks to Newkirk, I could also see that they existed on a continuum. They had a meeting ground, and that meeting ground was a sense of an author's purpose guiding and grounding an argument for the writer and his or her audience.

## Argument-Based Writing as Entertainment

We might think of this as a sticky kind of writing, one where a writer's purpose guides an argument that binds him to his audience. Both are held together because—as I will argue in this book—this writing is entertaining.

For now, I want to answer three questions: What does it mean to entertain? What is writing that entertains? How can writing that entertains be argument based?

What does it mean to entertain? To entertain is to play. For example, popular entertainers play: they play basketball, musical instruments, and so on. When I play, as philosopher John Dewey (1916) writes, my "activity [becomes]...its own end" (238); that is, I become one with a subject matter that, as a result, becomes my "object-to-think-with" (Papert 1993, 23). Where does the musician end and the guitar begin? We really can't say, but in the end, the guitar player isn't a musician unless she has her instrument. They are related, and their relationship is not static, either. Playing the opening bars of Deep Purple's "Smoke on the Water" is hard for a novice, but a veteran must go further, using basic and advanced rules with increasing flexibility. Like this guitar player, when I play, I am purposefully struggling with materials that resist me, changing me as I change them, in pursuit of an equilibrium—a work of art. To entertain, then, means to hold something close. The statement "it is important to *entertain* alternatives" reflects this. But to entertain also means to perform an act that is not entirely rehearsed. When I say, "Let me *entertain* you," I am speaking of this performing aspect of entertaining. Holding and performing—the two halves are always there; in the performing sense, I may be entertaining you, but if what I'm doing is worthy of the name, I need to be enjoying it, too.

To entertain, then, means to purposely hold something close and arrive at an unexpected equilibrium: a performance.

It may be easy to use a philosopher who argued people—students, artists, critics, everyone—learn by experience to analyze what it means to entertain. There are other sources, too, though, that present a similar view. The *Oxford English Dictionary* (or *OED*) defines the verb "to entertain" in five ways:

1. To hold mutually; to hold intertwined.
2. To maintain, keep up.
3. To maintain relations with.
4. To hold engaged, provide occupation for.
5. To find room for; to give reception to.

Definition 4 is the one that reflects what we think of when we think of popular entertainers, who definitely "engage" and "occupy" spectators. The performing aspect of entertainment is reflected here. Definitions 1 and 5 reflect the "holding close" aspect of entertainment, where the artist "give[s] … reception to" an object so deeply that each has the potential to reshape the other—a "mutual" intertwinement. Definitions 2 and 3 are a kind of umbrella for the others—saying, in a sense, that there is oneness, relatedness here: between player and instrument, entertainer and entertained.

## What Is Writing That Entertains?

When most people think about entertaining themselves, they do not start writing papers. I know I certainly do not. It bears mentioning that writing systems were developed by rich, powerful people for the purpose of what writing historian Andrew Robinson calls "accountancy," or to keep track of their stuff—to do nothing but record what exactly was there so they could use it as they saw fit. The earliest form of "proto-writing" we can find is the Sumerian fired clay tablet, which scholars currently date to 3300 BC. Here is how Robinson (2009) narrates the development of this recording system

> [S]ome time in the late 4th millennium BC, in the cities of Sumer in Mesopotamia—the "cradle of civilization" between the rivers Tigris and Euphrates—an expanding economy compelled the creation of writing. The complexity of trade and administration reached a point where it outstripped the power of memory among the governing elite. To record a transaction in a dependable, permanent form became essential to government and commerce. Administrators and merchants could then say the Sumerian equivalent of "I shall put this in writing" and "Can I have this in writing?" (8)

So, from the beginning, writing could be used to objectify—to control things and (as in the case of the administrators, slaves, etc.) people. This controlling function of writing was not weeded out with the development of formal language instruction, either, as, for example, the rise of English as a field of study, narrated by Terry Eagleton (1983), makes clear. When absolute authority began to founder in nineteenth-century England and the wealthy needed to provide evidence to justify their privilege, "state-established schools" were opened to "transfus[e]" their values ("the 'best culture of the nation'") as a means of "controlling and incorporating the working class" (24). The "accounting" function of language survived the rise of formal language instruction, and it remains today. Still, writing can be a form of entertainment, and when it is, we have a way out of this vicious cycle, because in this moment, writing is not a record but a relationship. Unfortunately, accepting that writing = entertainment gets more difficult as we move from more expressive to more transactional texts. As far as the most expressive ones go, think "summer reading"; think genre fiction; think binge watching the television series *Orange Is the New Black* or *BoJack Horseman*. Starting even here, we see that arguments are being made. Let's look at an example from a Trader Joe's Fearless Flyer (2017), a description of the store's White Cheddar Corn Puffs:

> These Puffs are made just for us with cornmeal that's combined with water and baked to a light, airy, yes, puffy texture, then generously coated with powdered white Cheddar that's (gasp!) made from *actual white Cheddar cheese*! True story. They're made in TJ's Too Secret Corn Puff Machine No. 00358. (Not so true story. But the idea of it is great, and we even emblazoned the bag with a very detailed picture of what that machine might look like.) You've likely had "cheese puffs," but unless you've had ours, you've never had the World's Puffiest. They're really cheesy, and that separates them from their less puffy counterparts.

We would expect an advertisement to praise its product's quality. This one does, including a logical appeal: that Trader Joe's corn puffs are made with real cheese, a special characteristic relative to most similar products. So, there is a typical transactional move here—an argument, a position with evidence to back it up. There is more going on here, though. For example, there are at least two stories being told here. One is of Trader Joe's as a countercultural grocery store that is fighting the racket that is today's proliferation of "food-like substances" (Pollan 2008). Trader Joe's has character: higher-quality ("really cheesy") products than mainstream stores and an ability to perform incisive critiques of the world they dominate (noting how consumers are hoodwinked with chemicals by the other guys, distinguishing fact from fiction). The other story is similar: there are countercultural consumers who are as smart as Trader Joe's are. This is expressive writing, then: two parallel tales of "conflict" and "extrication" (Gottschall 2012, 186). These parallel stories are undeniably fun to read—with Trader Joe's and their customers coming off as corn-puff-baking and -eating heroes, David versus Goliath. These stories are not just here for fun, though. They are additional evidence for the "buy this" argument—in this case, ethical appeals, evidence that people with character make and buy *these* puffs.

So, what is writing that entertains? The easy answers that rule transactional writing out don't stand up. Novels, movies, video games: these are all stories, and stories—as we have seen—help make arguments and sometimes *are* arguments. Expressive writing can be transactional, and transactional writing expressive. Expressive writing can be entertaining, for author and audience alike, and the same is true of transactional writing.

## How Can Writing That Entertains Be Argument-Based? Turning to Rhetorical Theory

If writing that entertains an author and his or her audience can be argument based, then it's unnecessary for students to experience transactional writing as a waste of time. Entertaining transactional writing should not be an ideal—it should be ordinary, a taken-for-granted fact of every setting wherein transactional writing is taught and learned. Students and teachers need to expect that transactional writing must always be a search for knowledge—serious play, a blissful leap.

I do not make this argument in a vacuum, as a cursory look at insights on being a good speaker or writer from the Western classical tradition shows.

What does it mean to be a good rhetor? It's the same kind of search; (a speaker or writer) using signs (usually words) to persuade (an audience). What is comforting is how much agreement there has been on this for the past 2,500 years. As rhetorical theorist Ross Winterowd (1994) points out, "[t]he history of rhetoric and the emergence of composition can be traced pretty much in terms of the idealist-empiricist dialectic," which he explains this way: either persuasive language use is inspired or "'available only to the eye of the mind'" or discovered, the understanding being that "the materials of art are 'out there,' and art imitates, reproduces, mirrors" (2). So, good writing is either an internal search or an external one. These days, the latter perspective ends up being framed as the only defensible one. I mean, we don't invent language from the ground up, do we? Effective communication requires that neologisms, or new words, be rare. For these two views, I think the important conclusion is accepting the following:

1. A good rhetor must be a knowledge-seeker (the internal view).
2. A good rhetor has an art, methods she or he uses to discover more knowledge (the external view).

The first conclusion comes from Plato—specifically, his major works on rhetoric, *The Gorgias* and *The Phaedrus*. In the former, he argues the art of rhetoric—as it can make the "lesser cause seem the greater"—is a vice, "flattery" that distorts and conceals the truth. Flattery is something that "pretends to be that which she impersonates: and having no thought for what is best, ... regularly uses pleasure as a bait to catch follow and deceive ... it into believing that she is of supreme worth" (1990, 73). So a rhetor deceives, and she or he deceives not specialists—who do know what is best ("what is right or wrong, noble or base, just or unjust" (70))—but ordinary people. So, Plato, I think, puts his view in *The Gorgias* most usefully here: the rhetor "has no need to know the truth about things but merely to discover a technique of persuasion, so as to appear among the ignorant to have more knowledge than the expert" (1990, 70). Plato, using Socrates as his speaker, argues that he uses another method of argumentation: dialectic. In Plato's view, dialectic refuses to make the "lesser cause seem the greater," with Socrates saying "What kind of man am I? One of those who would gladly be refuted if anything I say is not true" (68). Dialectic, then, is a method that doesn't have a preselected position to which it is committed. If that is what dialectic is, though, Plato-as-author appears to be a rhetor, albeit one who eschews the idea of making the "lesser cause seem the greater." How is that possible? How can a rhetor's position never be wrong? If it is divinely inspired, a point Plato makes in his later work, *The Phaedrus*, where he says "the wise man should exert not for the sake of speaking to and dealing with his fellow-men, but that he may be able to speak what is pleasing to the gods" (90).

Although Plato consents that there are indeed textual characteristics of a "good speech" ("know the truth about the subject that you speak or write about it: that is to say, ... isolate it in definition, and ... understand how to divide it into kinds" and "have a corresponding discernment of the soul" (93)), refusing to call that rhetoric, it falls to Aristotle to clarify these abstractions and declare them a teachable, learnable art. Among other things, Aristotle first argues rhetoric is not "flattery"—a manipulative technique that frees a speaker from the "need to know the truth about things"—but a different kind of discipline. As George Kennedy (1999) writes, rhetoric is one of the "'tool' disciplines (*organa*) that have no specific subject matter of their own but are methods for dealing with many subjects." For my purposes, the idea here is that rhetoric is an object-to-think-with, an external type of knowledge that is a path to more. This external, empirical quality of rhetoric is evident also in Aristotle's (1990) definition of the art, which is "to find out in each case the existing means of persuasion" (119). The means are out there to be found. Second, unlike Plato—who emphasizes how rhetoric may distort the truth—Aristotle emphasizes how because it may be used by the unethical to sway opinion, rhetoric is necessary so that the good may prevail. As he puts it here:

> But since the whole business of Rhetoric is to influence opinion, we must pay attention to it, not as being right, but necessary; for, as a matter of right, one should aim at nothing more in a speech than how to avoid exciting pain or pleasure. For justice should consist in fighting the case with the facts alone, so that everything else that is beside demonstration is superfluous. (158)

Though good writing is inspiration for Plato and an art for Aristotle, neither questions the stability of reality, of truth. There is where the sophists come in—and give a great explanation for why rhetorical methods are so generative. So, neither Plato nor Aristotle questions the stability of what we perceive—either "in here" or "out there." That's kind of encouraging (*it is there to be found*), but it also comes to an end (if you find it, that's it). From a sophistic perspective, what—even how—we perceive is unstable. This creates, in John Dewey's words, a "problem" and a "possibility": truth is always on the move (so it's difficult to catch), yet to the willing, there will always be more to see and say about it (creating a need to keep going and lowering the stakes if one "gets it wrong," as what's wrong one day may be right the next). Thus, building on Plato and Aristotle, the sophists argue a third view of rhetoric:

3. A good rhetor's methods are a path to making new knowledge because using them (as a speaker/writer or audience member) means questioning perceptions assumed to be flawed to form new ones.

Protagoras, an early sophist, argues that "*man is the measure of all things, of things that are as to how they are, and of things that are not as to how they are not.* ... This does not assert that things in the world have no objective reality; rather, it means that our individual sensations of these things are all we can know of them" (Murphy and Kutula 2003, 34). In the sophistic view, lacking the means to know the absolute, we get as close as we can by entertaining dynamic, imperfect representations thereof, such as paradoxes (Gorgias) and stases (the idea that "there are at least two sides to every dispute" (Murphy and Kutula 2003, 34). Speaking well, thus, becomes a fruitful, unending quest: for some, its own "end" (Quintilian 1990, 323), and for others, a way of engaging with thorny civic problems (Isocrates). For Quintilian, being a good rhetor means pursuing what is "honorable," which sounds a lot like Plato; for Quintilian, though, writing on this topic is like piloting a ship where "scarcely a navigator" has gone, an act of "what we may call cautious daring, to try that for failure in which pardon will readily be granted" (347). The reality we perceive is a moving sea, and embracing that—as the paradoxical phrase, "cautious daring," shows—is instrumental to writing well.

This sophistic insight has not left rhetorical training since the Greek era. Consider this typical advice from a popular handbook: "A thesis should take a position that needs to be explained and supported. It should not be a fact or description" (Hacker and Sommers 2015, 108). An indisputable "fact" will not do, allowing no room for reasonable disagreement. That is to say, a good argument must be one that may fail. So, the speaker or writer must consider what rebuttals he or she may face. Why would someone disagree with me? How would he or she use—or value—the same evidence I have? Questioning perceptions is abstract thinking made concrete.

## Going Small to Go Big: Entertaining Academic Writing as Fruitful Chase

Pursuing something that resists, good writing can—and should be—entertaining: a transformative act done for others and also for you. There is a choice to be made here, then, and that choice is yours: you can choose to be like Quintilian, to write with "cautious daring," or you cannot. Thankfully, being entertaining is your ace in hole. Why? Because good writing is Epicurean. To repeat an earlier point, truth is always on the move (so it's difficult to catch) yet to the willing, there will always be more to see and say about it (creating a need to keep going and lowering the stakes if one "gets it wrong," as what's wrong one day may be right the next). So, try to entertain that truth. You have plenty of resources to think with (a written language, interests, topics, prewriting strategies, a teacher, or peers). Using them, get as close as you can to a topic—one you can say is somehow a part of your "lived reality." What is it *really* like to be here and now? That is your argument to make; no one else can do it for you. Will you make it? Or will you just waste your time?

It's not an easy choice. As you know, I made a different one in my freshman composition class. But if you refuse to waste your time when you are doing argument-based writing—here and now—you will join me on an amazing path. You will not accept that an education that prepares you for the future is enough. You will only accept an education that is useful today, tomorrow, and every day between now and that future, one where you learn by having experiences and reflecting on them.

We are talking about something much bigger than what happens when you write here. We are talking about good writing as part of a good life, where learning never ends. You will recall that entertaining writing means chasing an inaccessible truth—a search that, because it is never done, is generative. You have your hunches, but because you're limited (the sophists' insight), you keep going (Plato's), using the resources you have (Aristotle's). It's a fruitful chase that *starts right here and now*. Other writers on learning agree. For phenomenologists, who concern themselves with studying the essence of lived experiences, we only know what we perceive. Although our perceptions are limited (as phenomenologist Maurice Merleau-Ponty (2002) writes, "I am my body" (198)), we share a dynamic world with objects (including language) and others; as a result, our perceptions are also open ended, paths to new insights (again, Merleau-Ponty: he is an ongoing "project" (434)). How do we chase that inaccessible truth as best we can? One thing we can do is write-to-entertain. We can ask questions like this: What does it mean to be you? To be a student at this school, at this time? To be a resident of your hometown? Life on one street is not the same as life on the next. The same is true of our online lives. Why is Myspace so yesterday and Facebook still relevant? Just any social networking site will not "do" in the same way. For phenomenologists, understanding the meaning of lived experience begins precisely where we bracket the "taken for granted" with "making the strange familiar and the familiar, strange." Like the sophists, phenomenologists assume there is more to reality than what we see at first glance. Phenomenology's gift is to tell us where to turn to see it, and that is in the minutiae of our lives. To return to an old example, why is that cheddar-and-bacon cupcake so good? That's where a good life—and good, entertaining writing—begins. Progressive educators agree. To focus on one, John Dewey (1934), when we have "experiences," we are in an endless chase where we learn. He uses the example of a dog's life to make his point:

> The growl of a dog crouching over his food, his howl in time of
> loss and loneliness, the wagging of his tail at the return of his
> human friend are expressions of the implication of a living in a
> natural medium which includes man along with the animal he
> has domesticated. Every need, say hunger for fresh air or food, is
> a lack that denotes at least a temporary absence of adequate ad-
> justment with surroundings. But it is also a demand, a reaching
> out into the environment to make good the lack and to restore
> adjustment by building at least a temporary equilibrium. Life
> itself consists of phases in which the organism falls out of step
> with the march of surrounding things and then recovers unison

with it—either through effort or by some happy chance. And, in a growing life, the recovery is never mere return to a prior state, for it is enriched by the state of disparity and resistance through which it has passed. (13–14)

That dog is not a closed system, and neither is his world, our world—but that's *his* ace in the hole. Being open means having chances. As Dewey points out, one who "grows" seizes upon those chances. This is what an artist—which includes every entertaining writer—does. Dewey continues: an artist "does not shun moments of resistance and tension. He rather cultivates them, not for their own sake but because of their potentialities, bringing to living consciousness an experience that is unified and total" (15).

So, let me, for one last time, repeat myself: what is it really like to be here and now? That is your argument to make; no one else can do it for you. Will you make it? Or will you just waste your time? It's time to write-to-entertain.

## CHAPTER 2

# DON'T WASTE YOUR TIME, PART II

## (Reading to Write)

This chapter argues that academic reading—like academic writing—can be an entertaining act. Academic writing is entertaining when you use it to "occupy the heights"—to challenge your prejudices, to meet something halfway in purposeful, investigative writing-to-learn. Writing-to-entertain is, thus, a relationship, something beyond "you" that you use to figure out what you want to say. Entertaining reading-to-write is a relationship, too. When you read-to-write, you are motivated to learn about and meaningfully respond to a subject matter that interests others—the author of a source, the people who agreed to publish it, a subscriber, and others. What, though, does entertaining reading-to-write really look like? I answer this question in the first section of this chapter, turning to two events in my history as a reader and to reading research that helps explain their significance. In the chapter's second section, I present four note-taking strategies you can use to do entertaining reading.

## Reading as a Responsive, Social Practice: From John Steinbeck to Mikhail Bakhtin

Contrary to popular stereotypes, reading is a responsive, social activity. Let me turn to two moments in my history as a reader and some reading research to show you how. I learned that reading was a responsive act when I was assigned John Steinbeck's *Of Mice and Men* (1993) in high school. Because many people are familiar with this book, let me directly say the book concerns two ex-cons, George and Lennie, the latter of whom is mentally disabled. They are itinerant California ranch hands who hope, as George puts it, to be able to "live off the fatta the lan" together one day (14), but readers see a rigid class structure standing in the way. I remember reading this, having actually come to identify with the characters enough that I had begun on some level to read this assigned book because it seemed "real," to intrinsically matter to me. I did not anticipate, however, the climax of the novel. In that moment, Lennie unintentionally strangles the ranch owner's daughter-in-law to death, trying to comfort her but unaware of his strength. When George finds her dead, George knows Lennie will be the next to go; out of love, George kills his friend. This is a murder performed out of love, a paradox, what to a sophist would be a story worth telling because it's a situation that presents no easy answers. I can talk about it this way, but what you must know is that when I read this passage, I cried my eyes out.

Now, I will cry when something hurts or, frankly, is so beautiful I don't know what else to do, but never before had my homework made me bawl. I didn't have the language for what I was experiencing then, but I can tell you what happened: I understood that for something to be called "reading," you need a reader. Syllabi and religious services name objects, in and of themselves, *readings*, but they shouldn't. Why? The convention implies that a text means what it does regardless of what anyone does with it. But a text without a reader is not "read" at all. I had, in this moment, discovered that when reading is consistent with my purposes, I definitely make something, and it's something way beyond decoding a message, or comprehending what someone else intended: instead, reading Steinbeck at that moment made a slight adjustment in how I saw the world that remains undone today; I responded to what I read, creating what reader response theorist Louise Rosenblatt calls a "poem."

Now, according to Rosenblatt (1994), a reader can read like a scientist or an artist. A scientific, or "efferent," reading involves looking for information to use elsewhere; an "aesthetic" reading, by contrast, isn't motivated by a desire to "carry away" something (24). Like the efferent reader, the aesthetic one reads with purpose, but that purpose involves forming a relationship with the text. The result, the "poem," is a sense of what the text means to him or her that he or she can draw on in interpreting other texts, events, and people:

> Under the magnetism of the ordered symbols of the text, he marshals his resources and crystallizes out from the stuff of memory, thought, and feeling a new order, a new experience, which he sees as the poem. This becomes part of the ongoing stream of his life experience, to be reflected on from any angle important to him as a human being. (12)

Rosenblatt's "poem" is not the result of a passive reading. Her view is that aesthetic readings are the most entertaining ones, more entertaining than information-trolling "efferent" readings and pleasure-seeking summer ones: genuine cheddar-and-bacon cupcakes. Furthermore, they appear to be the product of an individual mind. Other reader response theorists take a broader view, seeing a reading as the product of an "interpretive community" (Fish 1982), which could be any group of people with a relationship with a text (a ninth grade class, literary historians, etc.). But a reader response perspective—social though it may be—does not concern itself much with social consequences, with the politics of literacy. And I can say the same of myself in my reading of *Of Mice and Men* that opened the floodgates. Despite the taboos, all I could see was that George's action was a thing of beauty. I didn't want to talk to anyone about that fact—I didn't want to reflect on it in writing. I saw reading could change me—an awesome insight—but that change seemed to end right there. Reading could be active, but I saw that in a limited way.

It took another experience for me to see that poems could be made in reading transactional texts, too, particularly when I knew I was reading-to-write. I was in graduate school, having been assigned to read what had been an impenetrable genre for me in the past: literary criticism. This no doubt had something to do with the fact that I had taken a course in this subject in my master's degree program. Literary criticism courses usually introduce students to multiple "critical lenses" (Marxist, feminist, etc.) and examples of such criticism. Students, then, respond to various poems and stories by adopting some of these perspectives throughout a course. It is a kind of buffet experience, where there's so much to cover that one ends up tasting a little of a lot and running the risk of understanding nothing particularly well. Students can also end up making bad arguments because they are trying to use all of the topics and themes associated with a particular type of criticism. In the effort to add all of the bells and whistles, points get lost. I was certainly such a student in my literary criticism course.

Now, five years later, I was reading literary criticism again—in this case, the work of Russian writer Mikhail Bakhtin (pronounced bock-TEEN) for a course on Bakhtin, race, and literacy. Having foci on race and literacy meant we were using criticism not to interpret literature but the lives of everyday people, the struggle to be an ethical, raced, reading-and-writing being-in-the-world. The stakes were different—at least for me they seemed that way. I was also in a class focused on a single critic's work—the equivalent not of a buffet but a sit-down restaurant. Because I had been asked to read just one author to try to understand social problems, I was in a position to read differently, more meaningfully, than I had for my literary criticism class.

And read differently I did. Early in the term, my professor, Dr. Tim Lensmire, assigned selections from Bakhtin's work explicitly on language, *The Dialogic Imagination* (1983). In this book, among other things, Bakhtin shows he is a contemporary sophist, or someone who believes language—and meaning—are social constructions, products of human efforts to make sense of lived experience that, in turn, shape what we see and how we see it. Bakhtin talks about this back-and-forth view of language use as a dialogue. It's a nice metaphor, too, as it emphasizes how each literate act is an exchange with consequences, for writers and their readers, for those readers again when they start writing about what they have read, for their readers, and so on. Every interaction matters, and some matter a lot, becoming, as Bakhtin puts it, "internally persuasive," or moments when we say, "I agree with you" or "that's what *I* think." Reading *The Dialogic Imagination* was interesting to me, giving me a metaphor for language as a social construction that stuck. This did an important thing for me: I could see that Rosenblatt's idea that "aesthetic" readings were an entirely different species from "efferent" ones was problematic. That is, reading for information could mean creating "poems," too—could be every bit as entertaining. But I had yet to experience that fact.

That changed when I was assigned another Bakhtin work, *Rabelais and His World* (2009). In *Rabelais*, language use is not the subject; instead, it's how everyday people can revise authorities' ideas and institutions through the use of parodies. Here's an example: You know those candles in tall glass jars with pictures of saints on them? I once saw one dedicated to Our Lady of the Blessed Latte. I have never seen those candles since without thinking of the one praising coffee by taking a shot at seeking out favors from canonized saints. That's what parody can do, and in one moment, reading in the Walter Library at the University of Minnesota, I saw how Bakhtin's parodies, which had a radical, revolutionary quality to them, were another version of the dialogic relationship between readers and writers. Now, this might be hard to imagine, but I can remember getting that insight—seeing that similarity—for the first time. It was about 10 p.m. at night. I had worked all day as a writing center director and was now living my other life as a graduate student, trying to make sense of coursework that at times left me confused. Bakhtin may be more readable than some critics, but he's no picnic. All of a sudden, I felt like I crossed a threshold, that I was reading two books at once, that I had a lens I could apply to every page I saw, almost anticipating what was to come. I felt powerful, as if I had a tool I connected with profoundly, that made sense to me, that I could use to better understand myself, the people I knew, the other books I might read, participants I might study, and students I might teach. It was an exhilarating vista I saw before me, yet I was also silent, in a room of strangers who were probably half asleep. I should have been, too, but I wasn't; I felt as sharp as I had ever felt in reading a challenging text. I kept going for a while, writing notes feverishly in the margins—skipping pages, sometimes—continuing to see that connection between parody and dialogue. I continued for about fifteen minutes, celebrating by myself, soaring, until I felt with confidence I needed to go no further that night. I closed my book and walked out into the night, ringing like a tuning fork.

That experience was a lot different from the one I had had with *Of Mice and Men*. I was silently excited in both moments, but in the first, mine was a private joy. I felt responsible to do nothing else but try to be a more empathetic person. My second experience left me in a very different place, with an insight I knew I had gleaned from a tradition of democratic thinking, which I found I agreed with, and wanted to—as a writer, as a person—join and possibly advance. This was reading as a responsive act, but it was also something more, an understanding of reading as a social practice.

A practice perspective on reading introduces more than the idea that language—and reading—are social constructions. In emphasizing the idea of reading as doing something in the world, a practice perspective makes explicit that readers: (1) share a world (so what they do with texts has an environmental impact); and (2) belong to groups guided by values that may—and may not—promote the welfare of ordinary people. James Gee's (1996) idea that to read is to construct an identity as a recognizable "kind of person" is useful here (26). Having a style stops being an expression of individuality and becomes a form of belonging to a group. To provide an example of style as a kind of belonging, the Birkenstock sandals I wear are more than a fashion choice. Wearing them says I am concerned about my environmental footprint. I bought my Birks in part because they could be easily resoled; because they're also an expensive first-world-made product, I take them to my cobbler as many times as I can. So these shoes are not just a purchase I made once and have since used without consequence for anyone else. They are part of an ongoing relationship between the Plattsburgh Shoe Doctor and me. He's a cobbler, and I'm not, but he and I are networked, part of a group of people who are trying to keep old shoes in action for as long as possible. Together, and along with everyone else who gets their shoes resoled, we are countering the environmentally destructive idea (and group that believes) that having a big collection of the newest shoes on Earth is a goal worth pursuing. Wearing a shoe is about a lot more than just wearing a shoe; it's a social practice, an act that advances the interests of one group that coexists among others, all of which act with consequences.

Ringing like a tuning fork in the Walter Library, I knew my act of reading mattered far beyond my person. Specifically, I had an idea of how students who often resisted identifying with academic work could do so without losing their "street cred": they could respond to texts by remixing them, creating parodies that forwarded a group's interests. I have already argued how purposeful writing-to-learn keeps you from wasting your time because you are pressing on your prejudices and therefore actually *advancing* your interests. The same is true of purposeful reading-to-learn.

Purposeful reading-to-write can be done in a lot of different ways. I would like to use the rest of this chapter to describe several approaches to reading-to-write transactional texts. I include a few because every reader is, to some extent, unique. My belief is that the most purposeful reading-to-write is strategic. It has an aim, an end, so when it encounters an idea that it might want to draw on, that idea is no longer independent from that reader. A relationship exists, and there's a certain symmetry to it. A text has an argument to make, but so does this reader, even though she or he only has hunches about what it might be right now. For the moment, I want to say this: if that reader uses the same old strategies for reading a text, she'll never know if she might have read any more effectively. That's a closed loop. So, your goal is to straddle that pleasure and bliss line—to keep how you read-to-write somewhat flexible, using what you believe works best while also occasionally trying out different practices. As you tailor what you do, you can be confident that you are reading-to-write in the most entertaining way you can.

# Entertaining Reading Strategies

### Suspecting and Deciding.

A good reading-to-write strategy is something I'll define here in this way: it's a system for recording responses to a text where you (1) informally identify and restate in your own words examples and/or reference points you *suspect* reflect its argument. Then, (2) you reread those responses to restate what you *decide* its argument is and select particular examples and/or reference points to show how it makes that argument. You'll note that in my definition, I emphasize one word above all others: a text's argument. The most efficient, fairest summary of any text begins with a statement of its argument (which can be either lifted from that text or, to be as fair as possible (ironically), written by you); the worst summaries ignore this advice, trying instead to catch "all of the important points" a text makes. The problem with the latter approach is that it includes no definite moment where you stop, reflect on, and organize your perceptions. Although this step seems, and can indeed be, difficult, it allows you to conserve your best sense of what a text you have read is all about—a sense that, I promise you, will begin to degrade as soon as you start doing something else (reading another text, eating a sandwich, etc.). If you're like me, you know what it's like when your memory of one text starts to get foggy, and you know you have to start rereading. You just wish you could make an accurate, rich statement about what it argues and how, but all you get is a few vague words that aren't anchored in any excerpts from the text. You hope it will be enough, but you know it might suck. You know it *does* suck.

There is one way out of this mess: Leave your marks and, from them, form an interpretation of what a source is arguing and how: suspect and decide.

### Note-Taking Media.

If you are working with a hard copy of your text, you can write directly on it. You might also want to take notes on a separate sheet of paper or, of course, a word processing document. A Google document works well for this purpose. It's free, always available, and easily modified, even allowing you to speak your notes onto the page if you are working with a smartphone. If you are using a digital copy of your text—like an eBook or a pdf—you can use a Google document to record your notes, but you can more easily write or speak your comments onto the file itself. Using the free version of Adobe Acrobat allows you to take notes directly on most pdfs. The Kindle app is also easy to take notes with. Again, too, if you are using a smartphone, you can either type or speak your notes onto the file.

*Strategy #1: Hjortshoj's Outline*

In the excellent textbook *The Transition to College Writing* (2010), Keith Hjortshoj describes an approach to taking classroom notes that uses a suspecting-deciding approach and can be usefully applied to reading-to-write. Doing your suspecting best, you want to follow your hunches at first. This may involve *previewing* a text (its introduction and possibly its conclusion may identify its argument; if there is an abstract, you should take a look at that for the same purpose). Then, either on your source or another document, start to write down brief, informal notes that aim to answer a question: "What is my source's argument?" You may underline or highlight potential key ideas or memorable phrases or write down five- to ten-word blurbs that describe a potentially important paragraph's point.

Once you are confident you know your source's argument, review your notes, and write that argument down in your own words where you'll be able to find it later (using the first page, a star, etc.). Then, once again review your marks, trying to identify major sections and short, memorable passages that reflect each section's point. This is a good time to erase, delete, or cross out redundant or unimportant marks. Using an "I, A, 1, a" format is not important. What matters is that you understand your notation system—what the argument, sections, and memorable examples/passages are.

Let me demonstrate how this reading-to-write strategy can help you. I have before me the first chapter of Nicholas Carr's *The Shallows: What the Internet Is Doing to Our Brains* (2011). From the get-go, I am expecting Carr to argue the Internet is doing bad things to our brains, but how much can a reader tell from the title? To preview the chapter, I look at two features of the book I recommend you also consult: (1) the praiseworthy reviewer comments plastered all over the book to get people to buy it; and (2) the prologue, which is a brief, story-based introduction to the source. The reviewer comments on the back of the book don't tell me much:

- "Eloquent." —*Chicago Tribune*
- "Riveting." —*San Francisco Chronicle*

You get the idea. When I read the larger versions of these other reviewer comments just inside the front cover, though, I get a lot more:

- "We are living through ... a backlash against ... attention dispersion." —Todd Gitlin, *New Republic*
- "Absorbing [and] disturbing. We all joke about how the Internet is turning us, and especially our kids, into fast-twitch airheads incapable of profound cogitation." —John Horgan, *Wall Street Journal*

So I have some idea from looking at these longer quotes what Carr argues "the Internet Is Doing to Our Brains": it's changing (and weakening?) the way we think so we can't stay focused on anything for very long. It's a thought, certainly, but I haven't read a page by the author yet.

To become more confident about what that larger argument is, I turn to the prologue. I underline a word or phrase that I think reflects the first main thought of the prologue; it's *McLuhan*. I see McLuhan's name being repeated a few times through the paragraph; that suggests it's important. I see Carr quotes him a few times, too—most notably when Carr says, "[McLuhan] was a master at turning phrases, and one of them … lives on as a popular saying, 'The medium is the message'" (2). The idea, here, is that a text's point is the medium it comes in (e.g., a book's point is "book").

Now, I ask myself, a question, "Did Carr quote this because it's famous or because it's related to Carr's argument?" I decide to run a test you can also use: Will the next sentence reflect the idea I think may be related to my source's argument—in this case, how "the medium is the message"? It turns out that in the prologue, I see McLuhan's idea reflected throughout. Here are a few lines from Carr that reflect McLuhan's "medium + message" idea:

- "Media work their magic, or their mischief, on the nervous system itself." (3)

- "We're too busy being dazzled or disturbed by the programming to notice what's going on inside our heads." (3)

- "The computer bulldozes our doubts with its bounties and conveniences. It is so much our servant that it would seem churlish [by the way, churlish means "rude"] to notice that it is also our master." (4)

That last line is the last sentence of the prologue, so I know that must be a meaningful breaking point. I restate it in my own words (integrating a little McLuhan because I am trying to understand what Carr's message is): computers as a medium change the way we think in ways we ignore. When I check this against the book's subtitle, "What the Internet Is Doing to Our Brains," I think I am getting a better idea of what this book's thesis is. Here's a stab at it: computers are changing how we think. I've moved beyond McLuhan, and I'm not even at Chapter 1 yet. That's what previewing can do.

Begin outlining attempt. Okay, I've got my possible thesis in mind; so, I continue to scout out phrases that seem to reflect the book's argument, such as "my mind would get caught up in the twists of the narrative" (5).

As you can see from my notes in the book in the photograph, I underline it, and when I do, I am thinking this: this book concerns how computers change the way we think.

As you should do at this point, I start to pivot away from trying to understand the book's argument to figuring out what this particular chapter is about. I keep underlining, but I also start looking for chapter sections, five to ten chunks I can meaningfully break it down into. Subheadings are helpful in determining these; so are transitions, such as one where Carr's examples switch from himself to others: "Maybe I'm an aberration, an outlier. But it doesn't seem that way. When I mention my troubles with reading to friends, many say they're suffering from similar afflictions" (7). At this point, I review what I've underlined so far and write myself a ten-word summary to describe the chapter up to this point on the margin of the page shown in Figure 2.1:

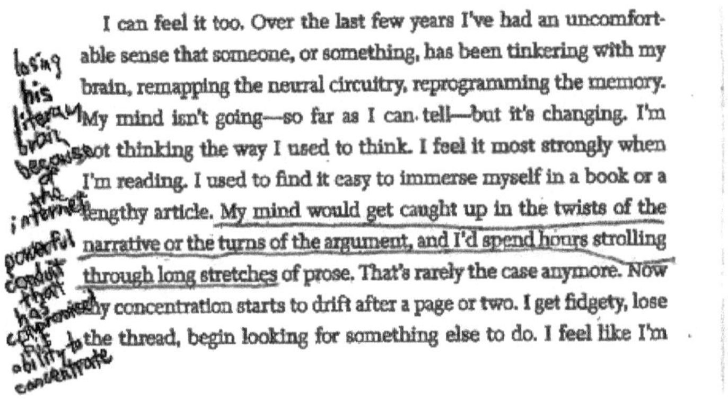

I can feel it too. Over the last few years I've had an uncomfortable sense that someone, or something, has been tinkering with my brain, remapping the neural circuitry, reprogramming the memory. My mind isn't going—so far as I can tell—but it's changing. I'm not thinking the way I used to think. I feel it most strongly when I'm reading. I used to find it easy to immerse myself in a book or a lengthy article. My mind would get caught up in the twists of the narrative or the turns of the argument, and I'd spend hours strolling through long stretches of prose. That's rarely the case anymore. Now my concentration starts to drift after a page or two. I get fidgety, lose the thread, begin looking for something else to do. I feel like I'm

FIGURE 2.1: The Shallows: What the Internet is Dong to Our Brains

> losing his literary brain because of the Internet, a powerful conduit that has compromised his ability to concentrate

This is a critical step you must also take when using Hjortshoj's strategy because it allows you to stay focused on what's coming next without losing any of your insights about this chapter so far.

Once you complete this process of underlining and section labeling for the rest of the chapter, you are going to have a decent outline of the chapter. For my part, I am able to look at them and ask myself a question: Based on the labels I've written, what seems to be the chapter's argument? This is what I write at the beginning of the chapter:

> Using networked computers has changed Carr's brain from a "literary," contemplative one (10) to a hurried one desiring and giving off "short … bursts" of information (10), a development that concerns him greatly because of the possible individual and social consequences.

When I look back on that sentence, one thought is on my mind: how much more descriptive a recollection of the chapter is this than what I could offer if somebody walked into my office right now and said, "Hey Tom, whatcha reading?"

In terms of challenging my prejudices about the book, too, note that when I began reading Carr, I thought he was going to say the Internet was gutting our brains. Now, at least in Chapter 1, I know he's saying it's a mixed blessing. That's way more interesting—it entertains me, has taken me some place new, so I am interested in continuing.

### Strategy #2: Behrens and Rosen's Summary

This note-taking strategy is also taken from an excellent textbook, *What It Takes* (2012). The strategy has a few more steps than Hjortshoj's, a fact that makes it a bit more directive—but also allows a reader to gather more information before deciding on what a source is arguing and how. Behrens and Rosen suggest that every text has sections, transitional points on which the text turns. These might be identified by subject headings or by sections typical to Western, argument-based discourse such as an introduction, division (or introduction of major points), first major point, and so on. I find it useful to ignore these headings when using Behrens and Rosen's summary strategy, as it forces me to think about what a section might mean. As you go, you may want to take marginal notes, but the essential step is to draw a line or insert a 1, then a 2, and so on, where each section ends. Keep going until the whole text is divided into sections. When you are done, review each one and, in about ten words, describe what each section's main point is.

Because this strategy is very similar to Hjortshoj's, I won't be as descriptive in my treatment of it, but I do still want to provide an example. A few years ago, I was reading Bill Bishop's *The Big Sort* (2009), a book that argues that post–World War II affluence has made Americans politically segregate or move to communities where people think like they do—a change that is diminishing our access to diverse persons and ideas. It's an awesome book, but as you can see, it's a book that makes a sophisticated argument. I draw together my notes from the beginning of its first chapter, "The Age of Political Segregation," right here:

### Section #1 (19–24)

- swerving at Harris (20)
- screwdriver (20)
- church-sanctioned "scavenger hunt" (21)

- Democrat and Republican lists (22)
- "party" metaphor (23)—it "feels right" (24)

*Section description*: As their increasingly extreme behaviors show, Americans are acting on lifestyle knowledge to politically self-segregate, to be among their "kind[s] of people" (23).

### Section #2 (24–25)

- don't cross-pollinate, but exhibit anger in "swarms" across party lines (24)

*Section description*: Politicians are also exhibiting increasingly extreme, partisan behaviors.

### Section #3 (25–28)

- 70% extreme views on abortion (26), while "somewhat" position "shriveled" (26)

*Section description*: Although some critics have asserted Americans aren't polarized but react to a partisan elite, Bishop holds that not only has Americans' "ideological allegiance" grown since the 1970s but also that their contemporary geographic segregation proves this polarization is a reflection of popular will (27).

As I went through the chapter looking for major sections, I underlined and wrote brief marginal notes where important points stood out to me; these are the bullets you see above. The section descriptions are very much like the ten-word summaries from the Hjortshoj strategy; the only major difference is that I had all of my sections identified before I started writing the descriptions up. Once I had written them for all of Chapter 1's sections, as with Hjortshoj's approach, I had a list of descriptive statements I could study to determine Bishop's chapter's argument. I include it here:

> Bishop and Cushing found multiple measures revealed America's political segregation to be a national fact—a fact the cultural consequences of which remain unclear.

Once you have a thesis for a chapter written in your own words, you can draw on your section descriptions to provide a brief summary of the text. It is really this simple:

1. Begin with the chapter's thesis;
2. list the section descriptions; and

3.  with each section description, pair brief examples/passages from the text.

You'll be off to a great start.

*Strategy #3: Phenomenological Themes*

This approach is slightly more directive still than Behrens and Rosen's. Its real strength is that it keeps you from thinking your source has made *the* authoritative statement about your topic. When you write notes to create phenomenological "themes" (van Manen 1990), you are researching the "essence" or invariant properties of some kind of lived experience. You want to first consider what phenomenon you are researching, whether it is being a first-year student, how your hometown's politics are reflected in the culture of your high school, or something else. The more specific you are, the better, but the important thing is being able to name your phenomenon. Second, you turn to your sources, which should be primary (first-person account) or secondary (interpretations of first-person accounts that may draw on other secondary sources, too) ones that *focus on the same phenomenon you are researching*. Third, as in Behrens and Rosen's strategy, you begin to mark off where a text appears to say something new about your phenomenon, which phenomenologists call a "meaning unit." Whenever the text starts talking about the next meaning unit put a slash (/); and whenever the text appears to not be focused on the phenomenon, cross out the material. Keep going until you are done. Fourth, review your meaning units, eliminating redundant ones and material unrelated to the phenomenon. Fifth—and again, much like Behrens and Rosen—describe your meaning units in your own language. Sixth, reviewing your meaning units, ask yourself this: what are the main points this text makes about the phenomenon? You should write down several in your own words, recognizing that several meaning units will often fit under a single theme. Seventh, and finally, once you have your text's themes, reread them to answer this question: What does my text argue the phenomenon is all about? When you have your answer, write it down. Identify or list your themes, pairing each with brief examples/passages.

Let me demonstrate this approach, too. In one study I conducted (Friedrich 2014) on writing tutors, I was seeking the essence of being a tutor in a particular writing center. To reveal this essence, I gathered tutor-authored accounts of the instructional choices (establishing rapport, asking the writer to orally restate an unclear point in her or his writing, etc.) they made in a session they had just completed. Here, I provide a brief excerpt from one of these accounts with the meaning units (step 3) identified:

I asked how it [the food paragraph] related to her overall argument / and she started talking about how rich people had a lot of food and poor people didn't in the novel. I told her that this was a good start on an arguable thesis about class. / She then started talking about themes and pointed out a paragraph that was about food and punishment as a theme. The themes also appeared in her thesis. We looked back at the assignment, / and it became clear to me that stating how the theme of food related to the other themes in the text was a huge part of the assignment. I told her that was what I thought, so that it was definitely good that she was sticking to themes. (Friedrich 58–59)

Clearly, a question about a paragraph's relationship to the argument and an offer of praise regarding the thesis are not the same instructional choice. That was a good place to insert a / mark. To move on to step 4, which involves deleting redundant or unrelated material, you can see I scratched out wherever the tutor was describing the writer's choices. I was only interested in teacher choices, so that was material I did not need. On the "redundant" point, you will note I eliminated part of the next-to-last sentence. Because it restates how it was good the writer was "sticking to the themes," I thought I didn't need the "theme of food" point. For step 5, where I converted the tutor's language into my own, I put this:

1. Tutor asked the writer to explain how this information supported her argument.
2. Tutor and writer reviewed the assignment sheet.
3. Tutor told the writer of this perception about food as a theme related to other themes in the novel as an assignment requirement.

With this done, I could move to steps 6 and 7, where the essence of the experience of making choices became my explicit focus. I noted a couple of things: (1) a flexible approach (the tutor asked questions but also stated an opinion); and (2) the tutor's desire to accomplish a goal. Flexible instruction, goal directedness: these claims brought me close to the center's essence as lived in individual sessions. More to the point, I had a succinct record of what one source said the essence of my experience was—themes I could keep in mind as I took notes on other sources. Using this strategy, you read for pattern, and hopefully avoid author worship.

### Strategy #4: Ketner Cards

I want to describe one more note-taking strategy, a strategy that is particularly useful with book-length sources. I call these Ketner cards, based on a conversation I had with a colleague, Jay Ketner. We were discussing how we had taken notes when working on our dissertations. I produced a book that had been important to me and opened the cover. Inside the cover, I had several pages of writing, including summaries of approximately ten words and examples/passages drawn from the book, with page numbers indicating where I'd drawn them from. There were often lines connecting related points and sometimes stars or circled page numbers indicating particularly important points. I also often put a statement of about ten to twenty words of the source's argument just inside the front cover, at the very top. Jay looked at my book, and then he explained to me how he had used a similar system; the only difference was that he had put his notes on a note card or piece of paper he had folded into fourths. The benefit of Jay's method as opposed to mine, of course, is that you don't have to own the book to do it.

There are two important things to note about the Ketner card method. You include the summaries and examples/passages as you work your way through the text. Then, to nudge yourself toward articulating what you think your source's argument is, either when you think you might be losing it or are confident you've got it, start drawing those connecting lines, or including stars or circling page numbers. When you are through, put down your version of your source's argument. Finally, it can be useful to use numbers or letters to identify main supporting points.

Let me include one of my own Ketner cards, which I wrote on a book I own, Lisa Wilson's *Ye Heart of a Man: The Domestic Life of Men in Colonial New England* (1999):

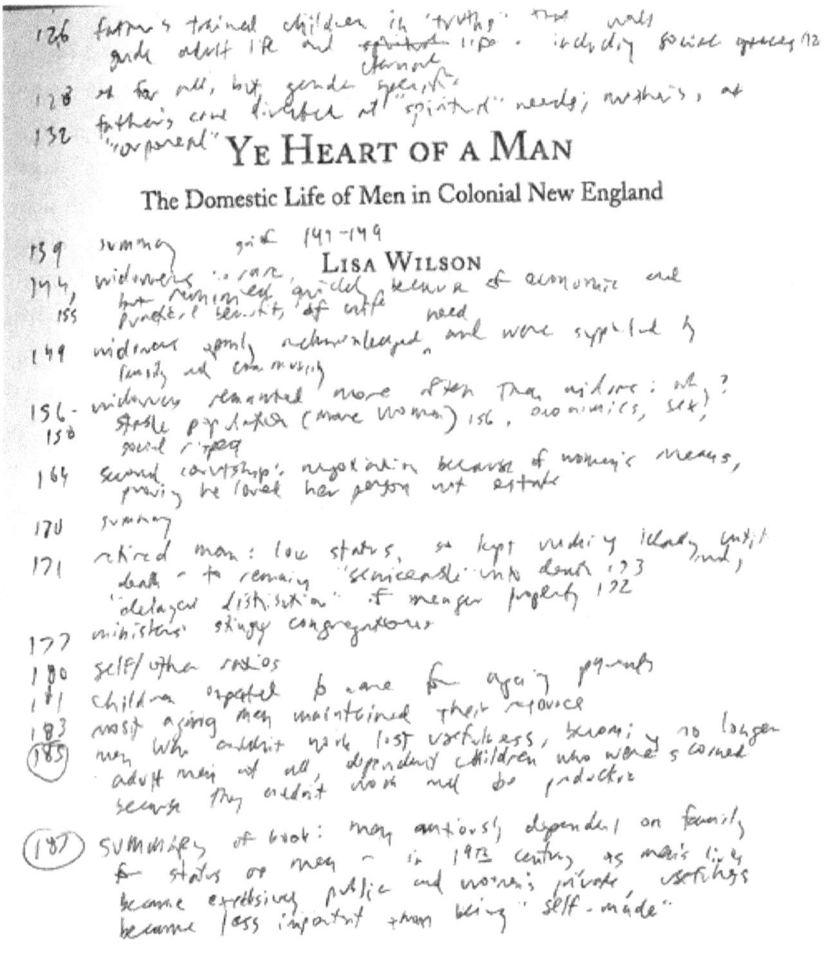

# Ye Heart of a Man

The Domestic Life of Men in Colonial New England

## Lisa Wilson

FIGURE 2.2: Notes written on "Ye Heart of a Man"

I want to draw attention to some key Ketner card features. First, every place where a statement stood out to me as important (reflecting the book or a chapter's argument, an idea I hadn't encountered earlier in the book or, for that matter, anywhere else, an idea I *had* come across somewhere else, etc.), I put down the page number and an informal comment, just for myself (a good thing, too, given my lousy handwriting). Second, note my circled page numbers at the bottom. Again, those are places where I was confident I had grasped a key idea. Third, I write that the last one is a "summary of the book"—but that is also not far off from its argument. Typed up, I write this: "men anxiously dependent on family for status as men [in the colonial era, whereas] in the 19th century, as men's lives became exclusively public and women's private, [the colonial man's sense of value based on] usefulness [to one's family] became less important than being 'self-made.'" The great thing is that I read this book about five years ago and had forgotten pretty much everything about it. Now, by consulting a few pages, I could meaningfully use it as a source in my writing. Think about that. It's an amazing resource: from "huh?" to "nuanced understanding" of a whole book in a minute or so. That's what you get from a Ketner card.

## Conclusion

These reading-to-write strategies help you draw a text close and perform what you discovered there by asking you to suspect and decide what a source's argument or its position on a phenomenon is. Now, if you've only ever read without taking notes, you will be in for some growing pains here, but they are worth it. Why? Because these strategies are designed to change you, to leave you more learned than you were before using them. Like a cheddar-and-bacon cupcake, they take you somewhere—an essential thing when you are reading-to-write and writing-to-learn with the goal of challenging and reporting on how you transformed your prejudices about a topic. Each crazy cupcake has its rules, and playing by them will have consequences. That's a good thing, provided you hold yourself to a standard: you insist on finding a topic that challenges and enthralls you.

CHAPTER 3

# ENTERTAINING WRITING ON EVERYDAY TOPICS

have made the argument that writing and reading can definitely be wastes of time and that if you do entertaining writing and reading-to-write, they will not be. Instead, you will make responding to texts in writing part of a life well lived, a life where you refuse to ignore your purposes.

The key to doing this work is finding your own cheddar-and-bacon cupcakes. I am talking about topics or strategies that attract you as a writer, even though you don't exactly know why—about familiarity with a twist. As long as your interests are driving you, though there is some risk, that twist also has special powers. It's a prejudice-challenging engine that can drive you, for free, to a new sense of what everyday life can be. However small, that's a way forward, an escape hatch, a portal to a new state of mind from which you won't be able to return.

To help you find *your own crazy* cupcakes, this chapter (and the next two) does two things. First, it provides you with a toolbox of strategies for finding everyday topics that are your own cheddar-and-bacon cupcakes. It starts you on the hunt by focusing you on a general, everyday phenomenon you know well: in this case, the experience of being a student. Second, this chapter demonstrates how the genres that university writing is done in present you in your Epicurean quests with everyday acts (e.g., how to summarize = to repeat) that occupy your attention while revealing knowledge that is hard to come by and essential to writing well (e.g., how an attempt to summarize = to reveal a source's argument).

## One Everyday Topic: Being a Student

In the developed world in 2019, compulsory, free public primary and secondary educations are a taken-for-granted fact of life. In the United States, it is literally illegal for minors to not be in school. This was made clear to me as a student teacher in an Iowa high school, as early in my term of service I often forgot to post attendance outside the classroom door after homeroom. My cooperating teacher discreetly let me know this was not simply creating problems for school record-keepers; rather, it told the police they did not have to track down a missing person. As this policy shows, universal public education is a right and a suspension of rights (I want to play Xbox, not go to English). It liberates and limits, and as the emphasis on high-stakes assessment grows, the limiting part seems to become ever more definitive of the experience of schooling. For my purposes, the limiting part of school draws attention to how it is patterned. Tests, periods, lockers, hallways, PA systems, bathroom passes, history classes: the list is infinite. There is a lot of consistency, such that schooling experiences in Iowa look like ones in New Jersey, Alberta, or elsewhere. That patterned quality of schooling also means that arguments are there to be made about what it is all about, not only in one school but many. That is to say, entertaining writing about a schooling experience is social from the start—a message worth sharing.

But we also can see that, once we start to list how schooling is patterned, we begin to see how to dismiss it as the same everywhere is to miss out on a lot of richness—on a lot of phenomena that we group under the general topic of schooling.

This richness of experiences we call schooling becomes particularly obvious once we start thinking about bodies being present in particular spaces and moments in time. In *Ecological Literacy*, David Orr (1992) makes the point that life in one place is simply not the same as life elsewhere:

> The campus as land, buildings, and relationships is thought to have no pedagogic value. ... A "nice" campus is one whose lawns and landscape are well-manicured and whose buildings are kept clean and [in] good repair by a poorly paid maintenance crew.

From distant and unknown places the campus is automatically supplied with food, water, electricity, toilet paper, and whatever else. (103)

Until you hit the line about the "poorly paid maintenance crew," a generic image of a school comes to mind. Afterward, we know each place is particular—for that maintenance crew member, this cafeteria eater, and so on.

This particularity in the student experience marks a rich entry point for writing-to-entertain. For when it comes to writing about student experiences, topics begin to appear when one takes personal traits and calls them particular student experiences. I am a white male from a middle-class, Midwestern family who attended St. Olaf College, majored in history, got a C- in calculus, never had an internship, did some opinion writing for my student newspaper, lived on campus in dormitories for the duration of my undergraduate career, and more. Let's go back to that C- in calculus. I took calculus instead of the course, "Math for Music Majors," because it sounded serious, and I wanted to learn something. But I quickly found out that calculus confused me, presenting me problems that seemed not like opportunities for inquiry but signs of my own incompetence. While I had walked into calculus curious, that quickly turned into a fear of math, or what mathematician and educational reformer Seymour Papert (1994) calls "mathophobia" (38). Now, being a mathophobe is clearly not universal. I'm not alone in it, but it is somewhat particular, too: a social phenomenon I know well. An essay on being a student could very well be so broad as to draw aimlessly on a few stereotypes and end up saying absolutely nothing of value. Having as my topic the experience of being a student who dislikes math, by contrast, would be much less likely to yield the same result.

The experience of being a mathophobic student would be a good topic for me to write on—a limited phenomenon of interest to me that I have experienced firsthand *and* one that others like Papert, care about, too. It's a convergence of purposes, a place where speaker and audience meet. Writing on a student experience that you haven't experienced can be a great choice, too; whatever experience you end up researching, you must be interested in the experience and, in the process of researching it, challenge your prejudices on what that experience is all about.

## Finding An Interesting, Focused Topic: Inventories, Taxonomies, And Possible Leads

But how can you arrive at a focused topic that interests you? Here are two types of strategies you can use: inventories and taxonomies. An inventory is a list of questions or categories that asks for informal responses from you for the purpose of describing you. A taxonomy represents—as a table, a list, a table of contents, and so on—an effort by someone else to categorize the varieties of a particular thing, such as types of birds, flightless birds, instructional models (workshops, lectures, discussions, etc.).

### Inventories

To find an entertaining topic, here are some inventories you could use. Your starting point for responding to any of them is considering what it was/is like for you to be a student at a particular place and time.

### Inventory #1: A Day in the Life

Choose a year of your life, ideally the present year, but another recent, important one in your life as a student would also work. Then, describe what you do/did on a typical day. As you list events, describe briefly what you did during that event, with whom you would do it, and why. (Because I don't like inventing personae to convince you I'm "like you," I'm just going to fill these out based on my own life.)

**TABLE 3.1:** Inventory #1—A Day in the Life

| Event | 10–15 Words about What You Do/Did During It |
|---|---|
| Waking up | Use cell phone alarm cock to wake up—usually play electronic (Air, Daft Punk, etc.) |
| Breakfast | Bagel, or, if I'm sleep deprived, protein (yogurt, egg, etc.) |
| Going to school | Take child to day care |

### Inventory #2: Personal Census

If you choose to use this inventory, you will want to think about your schooling experience in general, with an emphasis on recent times. The idea is to identify the associations that public records (government- or school-based authorities) list for you.

**TABLE 3.2:** Inventory #2—Personal Census

| Category | Status |
|---|---|
| Gender | Male |
| Race | White |
| Social Class | Middle class |
| Subject Areas I excel in | English, political science, art history |
| Subject areas I am weak in | Math (especially calculus), physics |
| Organized clubs/activities | Swimming team, band (trumpet), choir, study abroad |
| Jobs | Maintenance worker (grocery store, apartments), construction worker (fraternity house renovation), resident assistant, bookseller |

## Inventory #3: Your Stuff

Here is another inventory you can use to describe your life as a student in a particular time and place: What valued objects do you use as a student? In this case, as with the schedule inventory, you should choose a year of your life, the current year or another recent and important one.

**TABLE 3.3:** Inventory #3—Your Stuff

| | |
|---|---|
| Clothing | Birkenstocks (comfortable, legal requirement for being inside a building), sun hat (fight radiation because I've had skin cancer) |

| Object Type | Item and Why It's Important |
| --- | --- |
| Technology | Cell phone (check e-mail, manage appointments on calendar, communicate with colleagues and friends), watch (manage time when teaching), Google Drive (lesson plans, student assignments, etc.), ESPN (keep track of Minnesota Twins), etc. |
| Transportation | Car, bicycle sometimes (to get to, around campus), etc. |

## Inventory #4: Most Memorable Moments

Another inventory task asks you to list important events in your life as a student during a given period of time (senior year in high school, Western civilization class as high school junior, first week of school at college, etc.). Create a list of ten, briefly describing each item in fifteen to twenty words, writing informally, ignoring clarity/correctness.

TABLE 3.4: Inventory #4—Most Memorable Moments

| Event (what happened, in 5-10 words) | Event's Importance (15-20 words) |
| --- | --- |
| | |

## Inventory #5: What You Complain about When You Complain about School

This last inventory asks you to identify complaints regarding school at a recent, important moment in or time period of your educational history (difficult class, senior year of high school, etc.). Using either your own perspective or those of friends or family members, describe what happened and why it was a problem. You could use the following table if you were to consider a time in your educational history.

**TABLE 3.5:** Inventory #5—What You Complain about When You Complain About School

| Event Type | Why Problematic |
| --- | --- |
| Curricular activities | |
| Extracurricular activies | |
| Policies | |

Any one of these inventories could be useful to you in beginning to iden-tifying a purposeful topic. I recommend filling these out on a computer, as that will allow you to add table lines and add as much content as you would like. If one inventory doesn't help you generate much, try another. The idea is simply to start externalizing the educational past and present you have lived, so you can—by rereading—note what you've left out and would like to learn more about.

## Taxonomies

Another tool you can use to find an entertaining topic is a taxonomy. These comprehensive lists (including tables of contents, databases, etc.) may deal with any topic, including being a student. In terms of finding a topic, tax-onomies offer a vision of what being a student is all about that—impor-tantly—categorizes that perspective into labels. The labels that grab you are potential topics. In using a taxonomy for finding a topic, your goal is to see (1) an experience that interests you that is, as a result, (2) named in words that others (ideally published authors) use to describe a particular experi-ence (which means you can use keyword searches to find other sources on your possible topic).

### Taxonomy #1: Tables of Contents and Other Sources

It can take a long time to read a book, but it takes a few minutes to skim through a table of contents, chapter subheadings (like "Taxonomy #1," above), and index to figure out what a book contains in general. Well-written tables of contents and indexes will feature important labels (terms, keywords, etc.) used in a text. When it comes to anthologies and research handbooks on the student experience, these labels will imply—and directly identify—particular student experiences other writers have investigated. A useful anthology I've used in my first-year writing classes is Deborah Anderson's *College Culture, Student Success* (2008). Looking over her table of contents, student experiences begin to leap off the page: "*Steve Tesich,* Focusing on Friends; *Rebecca Dince,* Could Your Facebook Profile Throw a Wrench in Your Future?; and *Mindy Sink,* Drinking Deaths Draw Attention to Old Campus Problems." Student friendships, social media use, and substance abuse: Anderson's is a good collection, naming many student experiences. You can find her table of contents here (https://www.pearson.com/us/higher-education/program/Anderson-College-Culture-Student-Success-A-Longman-Topics-Reader/PGM217551.html). For some other useful places to turn, consider the following:

Advice guides for students, such as Harry Harrison's *1001 Things Every College Student Needs to Know* (2008). (You can view this online at the Amazon.com entry for the book; click on "look inside" on the cover image, then on the phrase, "table of contents," to the left of the book.)

Handbooks of educational research, such as Kristen Renn and Robert Reason's *College Students in the United States* (2013). (On Amazon, go to the book's "subject index." To give you an idea about what you'll find, here is a screenshot of the subject index's first page:

**A**
Academic advisers, 77–78
Academic biculturalism, 65–66
Academic preparation,
    190–191
*Academically Adrift* (Arum and
    Roksa), 205, 224, 232
Access to college: declining
    emphasis on financial aid to
    increase, 40; distance and
    online enrollment increasing
    feasibility of, 50–51; history
    of college admissions and,
    29–31; public policies
    pertaining to, 40–41
ACT scores, 191
ACT student surveys, 104
Admissions. *See* College
    Admissions
Adult students, 14

development of, 151-153,
207; campus racial climate
and, 102–105; college choice
factors influencing, 37;
college student enrollment of
(1976, 2000, 2008), 8t;
demographics of, 7;
discrimination of early
denominational institutions
against, 89; gender campus
climate for female, 101;
higher education history
and, 96–96; hours worked
per week by, 13; Posse
Foundation scholarships to,
72, 73–74; programs and
services to support, 108–110.
*See also* Historically Black
Colleges and Universities
(HBCUs)

**FIGURE 3.1:** Subject Index

Are you, as the second item in the list puts it, a bicultural student? A student with financial aid? Either of these could be great topics. Later pages have more.

1. Educational research conference programs, such as one from NASPA–Student Affairs Administrators in Higher Education. This organization's focus is on all aspects of student life on U.S. campuses. It has an annual conference. Page 20 of NASPA's national 2014 conference's program provides another list of potential topics:

**Administrators in Graduate and Professional Student Services**

266  Beyond the Bachelor's Degree: Revolutionizing the Philosophy of Student Support in Graduate and Professional Degree Programs

046  Engagement 3.0: Proving Online Support for a Culture of 24/7

034  Understanding Adapting and Re-defining "Graduate" Enrollment Management (GEM)

**Adult Learners and Students with Children**

442  Transforming Campus Culture: Creating Family and Child Accessible Institutions

126  Get a Seat on the Train: Reimaging the Commuter Experience

268  Building Communities of Support with Families in Higher Education

**African American**

005  Black in Higher Education: The State of the African-American Student

248  SistaDocs: Life After Graduation

211  Learning Communities in Higher Education

305  Actively Caring for People: Cultivating Compassionate Residence Hall Communities and Enriching Fraternity and Sorority Cultures

144  Strengthening Fraternity and Sorority Life on Campus: Lessons Learned from CSAOs

**Gay Lesbian Bisexual and Transgender Issues, Parent and Family Relations**

250  The Educational Experiences of Straight College Students with LBGQ Parents

368  The Future of Title IX: How your Campus Should Prepare for the Inclusion of Gender Identity and Expression

053  I'm Online: LGBT Identity Development in a Social Media Context

**Indigenous Peoples**

268  Building Communities of Support with Families in Higher Education

433  Responding ot the Call to Return Home: Harvesting a Decolonizing Practice in Native American Student Services Unit

FIGURE 3.2: Topics from NASPA—Student Affairs Administrators in Higher Education

These are the titles of conference presentations and the categories the conference's organizers grouped them into. Still, you can see potential topics here, topics spoken of in language you might even use to find additional sources.

*Taxonomy #2: Databases*

Databases are searchable, categorized digital collections of sources. Most people who have done library research have used one, such as LexisNexis (for newspaper articles) or Academic Search Complete, which my library's website states is a "Good place to start. Full text, scholarly articles on all subjects." What you may not know is that there are educational research databases, which you can treat as catalogs of student experiences—or topics (and, of course, sources). You want to remember that, at this point, all you are concerned with is finding a topic that is a cheddar-and-bacon cupcake: one that you connect with and need to know more about. That probably means not going to the sources you find, but reading keywords and skimming abstracts for the topics they bring up. Here are some valuable databases:

1. Educational Resources Information Center (ERIC). You can use this database (http://eric.ed.gov/) on your own, but a better idea is to access it through your school's library. Mine has it on EBSCO, which predicts keywords as you go. That is, if I type *student* in the search form, I get this:

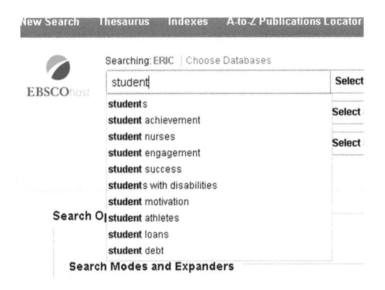

Your topic could be waiting there (what student does not begin college wanting to do well? Maybe "student achievement" or "student motivation" is your topic.) If you go a little farther, you will find even more specialized keywords. Running a search on "student motivation"—and adding a second search term that is useful in finding research that provides rich descriptions of student experiences (terms such as *ethnography, qualitative*, and *phenomenology* can all be useful there)—I found this:

8. Risk and Protective Factors in Mathematically Talented Black Male **Students**: Snapshots from Kindergarten through Eighth Grade

By: McGee, Ebony O.; Pearman, F. Alvin, II. Urban Education, v49 n4 p363-393 Jun 2014

**Subjects:** Urban Schools; At Risk **Students**; Resilience (Psychology); Mathematics Ach American **Students**; Males; **Phenomenology**; Identification (Psychology); Elementary Sc Middle School **Students**; High Achievement; High School **Students**; Charter Schools; Q Structured Interviews; Influences; Learning **Motivation**; Family Influence; Socialization; E Influences; Parent Role; Victims; Trauma; Violence; Neighborhoods; Poverty; Chronic Ill Mobility; Disadvantaged Schools; Ethnic Stereotypes; Stress Variables

Academic Journal

 Request on InterLibrary Loan    Full Text through LinkSource

9. A Phenomenological Study on Lack of **Motivation**

Educational Research and Reviews, v8 n16 p1369-1374 Aug 2013. (EJ1017166)

**Subjects: Phenomenology**; Learning Activities; Case Studies; Interviews; Undergradua **Motivation** Techniques; **Student Motivation**; **Student** Journals; Locus of Control; Qualit Foreign Countries; Attribution Theory

Academic Journal

 Request on InterLibrary Loan

10. **Motivations** and Enculturation of Older **Students** Returning to a

FIGURE 3.4: Ebscohost (2)

2. Although these results can overwhelm you with possibilities, more keywords are here, as well as sources you could draw on later in researching, for example, the experience of being a motivated male student.
3. Education Source. Find out about the EBSCO database (https://www.ebscohost.com/academic/education-source). Use this source in the same way as ERIC. While you are not in the business of finding sources yet, this database does, unlike ERIC, provide full-text access to the sources it lists. If your library does not have it, you can get a free trial.

*Taxonomy #3: Local Documents*

Your school also publishes documents you can use to find topics, including a college catalog and annual yearbook. Going to my school's catalog's section on "Student Life and Student Services," I find these and other campus resources: "Campus Dining Services," "Child Care Center," "Fitness

Center," and "Veterans Support." Do you ever eat in your school's cafeteria(s)? A paper on the experience of being a student on a dining plan could be a fascinating topic. Turning to your school's website can also be a useful place to look. One drop-down tab on my university's home page lists the following options:

FIGURE 3.5: Screenshot of SUNY Plattsburgh Homepage Source: http://www.plattsburgh.edu/.

Are you interested in getting a "Work Study" job on your campus? Do you have one already? That—and other options on this and similar lists—could provide you with a starting point. As with databases, though, your school's website can also overwhelm you with options. So, it is important to remember that your aim is to use your local source to find a topic that interests you.

If taxonomies and inventories aren't helping you find your topic, here are some possible leads, student experiences you may find it entertaining to research:

1. Being a first-generation college student
2. Being a student from a particular group (Native American, Chinese American, working class, LGBT, male, female, etc.)
3. Being a student who has a job
4. Being a student who has a child
5. Being a student with a learning disability
6. Being a nontraditional student

7. Being an ambitious student
8. Being a student who dislikes math, writing, reading, etc.
9. Being a student who procrastinates
10. Being a student who uses social networking software

None of these describes everyone. Still, each category describes a particular lived experience many students have in common and many in the culture consider important. That means your quest to be faithful to what your experience is all about will require entertaining others' perspectives on that experience. You must go on a prejudice-challenging, writing-to-learn journey.

Now, it's time to introduce some genres you can use to write-to-learn on particular student experiences that interest you: the rhetorical analysis and the phenomenological case.

## Genre #1: Rhetorical Analysis

In the Western tradition, rhetorical analyses can be traced back to ancient Athens, Greece, where ordinary citizens kicked out a tyrant and chose to rule themselves. The expression *mob rule* comes to mind, and the image it evokes is chaos. With this revolutionary act, the people of Athens created a unique situation: whereas the interests of all had—however well (or horribly)—been represented by a single ruler or wealthy class, ordinary citizens now had to represent themselves. Now, the idea of democracy we have is one called "representative democracy," where elected officials *represent* the will of everyday citizens (Hardt and Negri 2009, 254). This means that, for example, citizens of the United States are not welcome to go to Washington, DC, to propose and vote on laws. In democratic Athens, that is exactly what citizens did: trundle down to place they called the Pnyx ("Pnyx" *Wikipedia*) to cast white or black pebbles to indicate their preference for or against a measure. If you want to see an exciting account of this history, watch this perspective of ancient Greece (https://www.youtube.com/watch?v=G2tFo-Ta-i6w). But this "direct democracy" required other actions of these citizens (Hardt and Negri 251). They had to represent themselves in court and, in the marketplace, make arguments praising or blaming certain persons, events, and so on, in an effort to sway public opinion. It's easy to see how people who spoke persuasively had an upper hand. Thus, it's easy to see why a tradition of "effective symbolic expression" (Herrick 2008, 7)—or rhetoric—developed there.

We also know that when a person is persuasive, it is easy to ignore the moves she or he is making to create that impression. But those moves, down to the smallest gesture, matter because they are what a message is entirely made of. As a result, the Greeks wrote down what kinds of moves worked in particular situations. Still available today, we can identify, look for uses of those moves (what are called rhetorical topics and figures) in a text to discover what makes it persuasive (or not).

Because maintaining your interest in your task throughout is essential, you must analyze a work that deals with a student experience you genuinely want to learn more about. Having that interest means you will approach your selection with what I described in Chapter 2 as a sense of symmetry—a sense of investment in and developing authority about statements made on the student experience you are researching. That symmetry will guide you, haunt you, and make you know you need to be faithful to your topic, to the text you are studying. Your position on the persuasiveness of its argument will be your heart in your paper.

For Greta, the student whose example on which I will draw in this section of the chapter, that meant choosing to write an analysis of Thomas Oliphant's "Abandoned, but Not Alone." Oliphant's piece describes a foundation where LGBT professionals whose parents had once abandoned them due to their sexual orientation fund the higher education of students in the same situation. Greta wanted to know more about this student experience, given a prejudice she held and nearly everyone else does, too: the belief that parents' support (financial and otherwise) is essential. The idea of lacking that support arrested her, grabbed her interest. If she had been put in this situation, could she have made it? How important were parents at that stage in life? And could a person find a good parental figure if he or she lacked one? Reading Oliphant's argument made it possible for Greta to pose questions like these; in other words, she was reading-to-write about a text she identified with. Greta was entertaining Oliphant so she could entertain others on his persuasiveness.

But how to get there? She had two additional strategies she used to cross the bridge from initial interest in abandoned LGBT students to making an informed statement about how a particular text "worked" (or not): the analysis's generic features and appropriate forms of support that she could use to "mine" (Greene) a text.

*Strategy #1: Use Summary Writing to Determine Your Thesis.*
Much as a text needs to be read to be meaningful (Rosenblatt 1994), a successful rhetorical analysis must give its reader the information she or he needs to be persuasive. A rhetorical analysis often has the following features:

- Thesis on how a source is (not) persuasive with you, potentially touching on rhetorical devices it uses to achieve that end

*Source summary*

- Source's thesis
- Major source sections/points to demonstrate how it develops its argument

**Rhetorical devices' effects** (or how major source sections/points use rhetorical devices to be persuasive)

- Multiple paragraphs, each focusing on a device's effects

*or*

- Multiple paragraphs, each focusing on a major source section/point

*Conclusion*

- Tying claims about devices' effects to the thesis's (un) persuasiveness

As this outline shows, the bulk of an analysis emphasizes how the source text uses evidence to make its argument persuasively. An effective rhetorical analysis, though, is going to begin with a brief summary of the work being analyzed, beginning with some version of its thesis. Chapter 2's note-taking strategies can help you develop this summary; I suggest using either Hjortshoj's or Behrens and Rosen's approach. These notes can also help you see *how* your source makes its argument persuasively, giving you a map of *where* it makes that argument memorably. As you reread your notes, you can ask concrete questions like these:

1. Where were you first confident you understood "what she or he was getting at?"
2. What lines did you highlight there?
3. Why do you think you said to yourself, "I'm keeping track of that one" or "that's weird" or "sure, that reminds me of … " at that moment in the piece?

Without these notes, the *where* question will seem as abstract as the how one, but with them, you'll be in an entirely different place. In Greta's case, I want to show you how her summary led her to a focused, interesting sense of what Oliphant's argument is. Let me include her piece in full here. To illustrate my point, I am going to **boldface** the *transitional expressions* she uses to tell readers she is summarizing in a given place and to *italicize* her summary:

### RHETORICAL ANALYSIS

Today, being gay is still not readily accepted by society or more importantly, parents. Many conservative parents are still stuck in the 1950's where being gay was frowned upon and exiling gay children from the family was considered normal by the rest of society. Parental abandonment is still prevalent today, and through a group known as "The Point," these children are receiving aid through school and are given a mentor to see them along their journey. The Point was organized by a group of abandoned, gay students seeking to help other abandoned children and aid in the reform of the minds of extremist parents still kicking out their children due to their sexual orientation. In the article, "Abandoned, but not Alone," Thomas Oliphant successfully persuades me on his views of how the Point "keeps parents from undermining their kids' future" (27) by using emotionally developed examples such as the cases of current and former LGBT students and as well as the highly controversial conservative father who abandoned his gay daughter.

Having a conservative parent was never good news for any homosexual teen and Oliphant emphasizes this to show how parents may cripple their children's future through his almost "bash" of Alan Keyes. Thomas Oliphant uses such an example to make a clear statement about how he feels about these dishonorable parents. He wants the reader to know and understand his point of view on the issue of parental abandonment as a whole. Oliphant uses these examples to make the reader grasp that there is a problem in the world, and the Point is doing something about this problem.

**Oliphant begins the article** *characterizing Keyes as the "talk show noisemaker, the Republican pol, the conservative 'Christian' who abandoned his teenager because she happens to be gay"* (25). This automatically lets the reader know Oliphant's views on parental abandonment. It shows us an extremely relatable example of how there are parents who do undermine their kids' future. The fact that he uses a political figure to attack is also significant because it allows the reader to become more interested in the article if perhaps they may know Alan Keyes and what he claims to stand for. Oliphant states, "[Maya Keyes (daughter of Alan Keyes)] is anything but a unique case of a budding scholar instantly impoverished by vindictive parents on the threshold of life" (25), to convince readers that these parents of gay teens who decide to abandon their children are the ones trying to interfere with their kids' futures—not the Point organization.

**In the text,** *Oliphant uses the background stories of kids introduced into the Point and the kids who actually developed the Point* to evoke compassion from the reader. He depicts an incident in which a homosexual boy who was ruthlessly kicked out of his own home because of a diary describing his homosexuality that his father had found. Through this incident, Oliphant shows the almost heroic nature of the Point foundation in taking the boy under their wing after his abandonment. Oliphant also describes how the foundation was imagined and formed by kids who had been deserted by their parents in their past. He uses the quote, "They persevered, made it, and then made it big, resolving that they would use some of their wealth to provide the help that they lack" (25), to show the readers how hard members of the Point worked to become such a powerful organization and persuade us into believing that the Point's purpose is truly for the better of society. He wants us to see that the purpose of the Point is to help better the future of the kids it represents. From these two examples Oliphant is successful in showing the readers the true compassion and acceptance the Point stands for. He uses cases of kids who prospered through the Point to emphasize how the members of the Point are the ones out there looking out for the deserted kids. That it is the parents that force their children out of their homes that are the true issue in the world.

Oliphant is successful in persuading the readers that the Point's purpose is to help kids with their futures rather than undermine parents in their means of bringing up their children. He makes valid points in describing how the Point's purpose is only positive and only helps those who had already been parentally abandoned. Oliphant's use of sympathy arousing examples helps to allow the reader to fully connect with the article and understand the point of view that Oliphant is coming from. By evoking empathy and sympathy from the reader, he can grab the reader's attention and easily persuade the reader of his argument. I as a reader was fully convinced that the Point is meant "to keep parents from undermining their kids' future" through each of Oliphant's moving models.

One of the first things you'll note is that Greta does not summarize Oliphant's piece in one paragraph, and that is fine. If it helps you, you may; for examples of one-paragraph summaries, see Darren's procrastination paper later in this chapter. Greta does, however, something every rhetorical analysis writer must do in summarizing her or his target text: go on the hunt for its argument, because Greta can't say Oliphant has argued his position well without knowing his position. No dice. If we look for phrases that communicate "I am summarizing here," we want ones that do a few things:

1. Refer to moments in the text ("first, Oliphant," "the text, then," etc.)
2. Emphasize description (i.e., what you see) and minimize analysis (i.e., what it means)

Brief, memorable quotations are also useful, mostly because—at this point—they remind you of reading and saying, "that's interesting." Right here, let me draw together Greta's summary statements:

1. **Oliphant begins the article** *characterizing Keyes as the "talk show noisemaker, the Republican pol, the conservative 'Christian' who abandoned his teenager because she happens to be gay" (25).*
2. **In the text,** *Oliphant uses the background stories of kids introduced into the Point and the kids who actually developed the Point.*

This was an ordinary, brief summary, but Greta used it to conclude what she thought Oliphant's argument was. She saw the theme of abandonment in the title and the Keyes example, and she saw it when she looked a bit more closely at the "background stories," too. She saw a pattern that made her confident about a guess, as you can see from the first part of the thesis:

> *In the article, "Abandoned, but not Alone", Thomas Oliphant successfully persuades me on his views of how the Point "keeps parents from undermining their kids' future" (27).*

The idea of abandonment is here in how she includes the article's title, yes, but more importantly, in her decision to quote the phrase, "keeps parents from undermining their kids' future."

If Greta had stopped there, she might have had only a summary on her hands—and no analysis. What Greta did—and you could do—next, though, is seize upon that sense of Oliphant's argument and ask: where does he make that argument memorably? That put her onto asking other grounded, specific questions that reflected her sense that this piece was about fighting abandonment:

1. Where is this "undermining" being referred to in this article?

2. Where is it showing The Point to be a parental alternative?
3. How does this contrast between parental types make The Point seem particularly ethical?

Armed with this argument, she could easily create interesting questions that reflected her attachment to the topic. To find her device, the "emotionally developed example," she asked question a.), and went back to the start of the piece—to the arresting Maya Keyes story. Again, she looked for other similar examples in Oliphant's piece, and she could see she was on to something. She was writing-to-entertain in search of rhetorical devices at work, something you can do—too—by using analysis strategy #1.

## Strategy #2: Look for Classic Forms of Support

There is a huge number of rhetorical devices. If you want to see how many one scholar thinks there are, visit the excellent website, Gideon Burton's *Silva Rhetoricae (The Forest of Rhetoric)*. He lists hundreds, as do other authorities (see Richard Lanham's *A Handlist of Rhetorical Terms*, and you will see something similar). Unlike Burton or Lanham, I'm not going to be exhaustive here, but I do want to describe a few familiar devices the use of which often has an impact on a text's persuasiveness.

1. *Ethos, logos, and pathos.* These three do a pretty good job at describing among themselves the "kinds of people" writers try to establish themselves as in all discourse types: a person of good character who is "fair and balanced," has the interests of everyday people instead of a selfish elite in mind, and so on (ethos); a person who seems reasonable (logos); or a person who emotionally moves someone else—jerking tears, inspiring laughter (pathos). Because mixed arguments ("Although author x succeeds at ___ , he or she fails to ___") generally come across as the most mature, opportunities for saying part of an argument seems reasonable, but ultimately, a speaker who comes off as a scoundrel are worth considering. Or, a writer might have a reasonable point but fail to persuade you because she or he ridicules her or his opposition (or uses pathos too much). My point: yoking two of these together can really give you something.

2. *Definition.* Everyone knows definitions are a classic, often ineffective way of starting a text. But definitions are essential; without them, a text becomes jargon, a speaker seems uninformed or manipulative, and so on. You'll note that earlier in this chapter, I provided one for rhetorical analysis: "we can identify, look for uses of ... moves ... in a text to discover what makes it persuasive (or not)." If I had not done this, you probably would have thought, "What is this guy

talking about?" After that, hopefully you thought, "Okay. I get it." The power of a definition as evidence, though, is the opportunity that one included (or excluded) gives you to talk about what makes a piece of writing succeed or fail. That power is how definitions included—and excluded—reveal a writer's assumptions. Talking a lot about a person based on what she or he believes is easy to do.

3. *Metaphor.* These you probably associate with studying literary objects, but they make transactional texts work, too. Major ones for me in this text are the cheddar-and-bacon cupcake and the glazed donut. The first stands, as you know, for something you unexpectedly find appealing, attractive, and so on, and the latter, something you knew you liked in advance that leaves you unchanged. So, they are metaphors to describe what a prejudice-challenging writing-to-learn experience should be and do. My point is that metaphors can make texts beautiful, but they most importantly make the abstract concrete. They're useful to draw attention, too, because most texts use them—I suspect—because arguments are general, abstract things that rely on specific, concrete evidence to have force.

4. *Cause and effect.* One thing leads to another. That's not particularly interesting, but we use this device all the time and—often—what's assumed to be the cause of something sometimes isn't (as with the phrase, "bless you," a sneeze doesn't mean you're possessed).

5. *Examples.* This is a huge category, and it can often be most useful in an analysis when you think of a text's use of particular types of examples. In this textbook, for example, I draw repeatedly on examples from my history as a writer and a reader as evidence for making the argument that you should write-to-entertain. If you said, "Tom Friedrich uses a lot of examples," you wouldn't have much else to say about what I do in this book; if you said, "He uses examples drawn from his [that is to say, my] literacy history," you could talk about my writing experiences first and my reading ones second. That's a lot more material to work with.

6. *Authorities.* If you've ever cited a source you've used this device. It's valuable to think about because pretty much everyone uses authorities (so you'll rarely be disappointed if you look for how a text uses them to strengthen an argument). There are better reasons, though, for looking at how a text uses authorities. Examining how certain authorities are used—you'll note I am fond, for example, of John Dewey—and how sources can be out of date, politically biased, and so on, can be very useful to you.

7. *Statistics.* In our integrated world, it sometimes seems like the only thing that counts as "real evidence" is a statistic. (Think "7 out of 10 doctors recommend" or "GDP was up by 2.3% during the last quarter." Really, does anything else sound so authoritative?) To us,

maybe not, and that points to a big problem: behind each statistic is a methodology (Okay: you said "7 out of 10 doctors," but how did you define *doctors*? How big was your sample size? Did you control for cultural biases?). With a little prodding, it becomes clear how statistics can be created—and used—to deceive and manipulate. This can be a source of interesting arguments for you, particularly if you find a text suspicious.

8. *Counterarguments.* An easy way to argue that a speaker comes across as ethical is to point to her or his use of counterarguments— claims that support a view that is, at least in part, at odds with the perspective championed in a text. Any of the types of evidence noted above can be used to make counterarguments.

---

**FIGURE 3.6:** Analysis Outline

---

1. What is your source's topic and author's argument about it?
2. What does s/he rely on? Fill out as much as you can on the table.

| Type | | Example | How Might this be used as evidence for my argument? |
|---|---|---|---|
| **Varied Support** | Some of the types of support you may see include the following:<br>■ Assumptions (beliefs, possibly unexamined) held, ignored?<br>■ Definitions<br>■ Objections or counterarguments noted, avoided?<br>■ Cases<br>■ Analogies<br>■ Authoritative Testimony<br>■ Statistics<br>■ use of logos (being well-informed), ethos (being an ethical person), or pathos (being emotional in the sense of being patriotic, humorous, etc.)? Some combination? | | |

3. Based on the support you've identified, what are two arguments you could make about the source's persuasiveness? (Including your topic and thesis on the success of the source's argument?

---

I could have listed many others, but with just these few, you can imagine reading over a text and saying "there's a definition" and "hey, a counterargument!" and so on. As with the summary, this is a straightforward task that requires nothing but slowing down and closely looking at the piece of writing you are preparing to analyze. You do not need to be concerned at all about what your position on its persuasiveness will be in the end—and, in fact, if you are, you won't be learning much from what you're reading, anyway. At this point, you just want to collect evidence. Is its last point its strongest? That's a rhetorical device, too, called *climax* (http://rhetoric.byu.edu/Figures/C/climax.htm).

Once you collect your evidence, you can get analysis strategies #1 and #2 to work together. This is the time for, again, turning to your latest, best guess for what your source's argument is. You have a different goal now, though: not to construct a summary but ask how you see types and patterns of evidence being used in ways that make the argument stick for you. I have already suggested the types of questions you can ask at this point, so go ahead and ask, "Why does including a definition at point x (not) make this piece's argument persuasive?" If you prefer an alternative approach, I often use the form above, Analysis Outline, to have my students record their impressions of how support works to make an argument persuasive—and work toward writing an appropriate thesis statement for the analysis assignment.

Use these strategies to advance your purposes, and you will be in good shape. Greta might have referred to a wider range of devices—chances are, that would have made her analysis stronger—but by referring back to her thesis, you can see how she was able to reveal how Oliphant's argument worked for her—his use of "emotionally developed examples" to grab a reader's attention (Keyes's fame) and curry compassion ("Oliphant uses the background stories of kids introduced into the Point and the kids who actually developed the Point to evoke compassion from the reader"). From start to finish, Greta went on a prejudice-challenging journey. Parents weren't essential to college success, although a great boon to many, including Greta. Sometimes, though, they could be barriers, and in the case of abandoned LGBT college students, there was a way forward without them. That was a message that mattered to Greta, from start to finish. It was a chance to do entertaining writing. With analysis strategies #1 and #2 at your side, you can enjoy the same opportunity.

## Genre #2: Phenomenological Case

Another genre well suited for doing entertaining writing on the student experience is the phenomenological case. So, what is a phenomenological case? Let me begin by describing a phenomenological study. A phenomenological study must describe an experience in terms of its essential properties—those qualities that, if you were to look at many cases, would end up being there ideally all of the time. If it's done well, a phenomenological study will yield a description or set of themes that make the reader go, "that's it!" and as a result know more about an experience as people live it. In one phenomenological study I conducted on the choices writing tutors make in sessions (Friedrich 2014), I used themes. Composed mostly of undergraduate and graduate students, the staff I turned to for my data was very concerned about "getting something done" in their sessions. When little was, as one theme shows, a tutor might reach "a moment where s/he needs to tell the writer about a necessary revision or place to target in [a] draft" (63). Reading the theme evokes a sense of tension, of getting fed up with knowing better and not saying so—and when you read it, you know something about what it's like to be a writing tutor in that place.

To create findings like this, the phenomenological researcher works with two kinds of sources: what I will call "reflective" and "descriptive" texts. A reflective source is a secondary source that directly addresses what an experience is all about. If you are on a road trip with a friend, you probably won't say something like this: "I'm so glad we're on this road trip because, by being in unfamiliar places, we'll learn more about who we are as individuals in general and about each other as friends." Your friend is probably going to stare at or ignore you, maybe say, "Okay, sure"—and for good reason. The road is about being in the moment, not talking about it, and once you are talking about what it means, you are bound to be missing out on plenty. In that moment, you are a reflective source. Reflective sources typically used in phenomenological research include dictionaries (particular entries, including etymologies, or word histories), autobiographical accounts, and articles from academic or popular sources (ideally qualitative studies, which use systematic approaches to coding and analyzing observations, documents, and other data sources that are not numbers based). Descriptive texts are, by contrast, firsthand accounts—either spoken ("long interviews" (Moustakas 1995)) or written ("lived experience descriptions," or LEDs (van Manen 1990))—of an experience as it was lived. To return to the road trip scenario, a descriptive text would pile up stories of you and your companion battling over playlists and temperatures, revealing secrets because your defenses were down, and more. It's the report from the front line—unvarnished, uncensored, and just what it was like to be then and there. So, long interviews or LEDs aim to tell it like it was, not express the meaning of an experience many people have had. These descriptive accounts are the essential data of a phenomenological study, and a researcher uses them by looking for the themes of the experience that they report. The goal, of course, is to test prior claims or move beyond them, refining and/or adding to what we know about a particular lived experience.

The phenomenological case is one kind of phenomenological study. It asks you to engage in theory testing by reading reflective texts on an experience for the themes they say it is all about—and then testing those themes by looking for those a single, peer-authored LED includes. The goal in this instance is to say "after having considered this case, here's what we now know about a particular experience."

### Strategy #1: Stick with a Topic That Interests You

Like the rhetorical analysis, the phenomenological case presents you with strategies that make challenging your prejudices—or entertaining yourself—in writing an approachable, interesting task. As with the analysis, your most important decision is selecting a suitably focused, challenging topic you're interested in. This interest will ensure you have ideas about this phenomenon you can test against your reflective and descriptive sources' claims—a process that will keep you from wasting your time. While I'd like to mention that any of the "possible leads" listed above could work for a phenomenological case, the sample I'll focus on here—Darren's study of the experience of being a student who procrastinates—has an excellent topic, given that he'd written a rhetorical analysis of a source on this topic before (Paul Graham's "Good and Bad Procrastination") and was therefore aware that there were alternative perspectives on procrastination to be had.

### Strategy #2: Use the Genre's Major Parts

The phenomenological case has other strategies than the topic itself. The first of these is the structure of the genre itself, which calls for the following parts:

**Introduction**, where you possibly provide an example of the experience of concern to create interest in the case.

- Thesis: Although many theses (about this more later) draw attention to a conflict or paradox in the experience, any can be stated in the following way: "The experience of being a student who/with/etc. [name of experience] is … "

**Theory**, where you want to introduce at least two reflective sources that can arguably be about your experience. (For example, consider a source about working-class masculinity. This could be a work about masculinity, but it could also be considered a work about class, and maybe also about being a first-generation college student.) I suggest you treat them in one of two ways:

- In one or more paragraphs, present source #1's argument and a brief summary, followed by a brief list (two to three) of themes with examples of each in the work; then, beginning a new paragraph, present the same for source #2.

*or*

- In one or more paragraphs, present a theme covered in both/ either source #1 and/or source #2 (as they may not both touch on the same themes, although both present ones you consider essential to the experience), providing a source's argument when you first draw on it and an example of the theme drawn from that source; then, beginning a new paragraph, present the next theme with examples from both/ either source(s); and so on.

**Test Case**, where you want to draw on an ideally peer-authored LED on the experience of interest, including and providing examples of the person's experience of the phenomenon. The more descriptive your examples, the better; also, your quotes will ideally be the longest in this section, as rich, long quotes give readers a better chance to see what you mean to show; to judge that the theme you say you found in her or his LED is indeed there.

- Organize paragraphs by themes, using the same language you used in your theory section where you are talking about the same themes.
- Refer to how your reflective sources' themes are (not) reflected in the LED here.

**Conclusion**, where you return to your thesis, with the focus being on what we now know about the experience of interest based on the findings of your research.

Darren, in responding to this assignment, kept to this format fairly closely. Here is his paper:

We all have had a time where we have a certain task that we have to get done and we just keep putting it off until the "last minute" possible before a deadline. This is a problem people who procrastinate have to experience all too often. If there's one thing all procrastinators can agree on, it's that we know when we are doing it, we dread starting our work, and we know we shouldn't be procrastinating in the first place. We know we have work that needs to be done, but just can't bring ourselves to do it, even though we know we should; that is what being a procrastinator is all about.

Procrastination is something that can hold us back. It's not rare to have a time where you rush to do something and the quality suffers because of it. But it can also be something that can push us to excel; in cases where we have procrastinated to the point where we have no choice but to do the work. Procrastinating can hold us back, but that doesn't mean it has to stop us from doing well; though even when this is the case, we still know that we shouldn't have procrastinated in the first place. I think the essence of being a student who procrastinates is knowing we shouldn't be procrastinating but doing it anyway.

In the article *Good and Bad Procrastination* by Paul Graham, Graham argues that there can be many types of procrastination both good and bad. He goes into detail saying "There are three variants of procrastination, depending on what you do instead of working on something: you could work on (a) nothing, (b) something less important, or (c) something more important. That last type, I'd argue is good procrastination." (86) Graham is talking about how procrastinating always involves putting something off, but [it's] only good procrastination if you are putting off something less important in order to do something of significant importance. This, I think, is rarely the case, and most often we procrastinate for tasks that are more important in place of less important things. This would mean that in order to be a good procrastinator that we have to ignore and avoid less important things like chores and errands; these trivial tasks often get in the way of our real work. It's only when we ignore these other trivial tasks that we can buckle down and get important work done. Graham talks about how even though you may be getting things done, you can still be procrastinating. The importance of things comes into play and even though you may be crossing things off a to-do list, they may not be of the highest importance on the list. We have to prioritize our work. When procrastinating, it seems that things that may be of high priority are the ones that [keep] getting put off. It's only when we either force ourselves or are forced to work on the high priority things that they get done. As Graham says, " … it's easier to get yourself to work on small problems than big ones." (89) This is because we get satisfaction from working on small problems much sooner than we would from working on big ones. Bigger problems take more time, so the feeling of accomplishment is much further away; however, the bigger problems give the greatest feelings of accomplishment.

An article from the *New Yorker* by James Surowiecki entitled *Later* takes a more philosophical look at procrastination, and tries to analyze what procrastination says about us as people. Early on in the article Surowiecki says this about procrastination, "It's a powerful example of what the Greeks called *akrasia*—doing something against one's own better judgment. Piers Steel defines procrastination as willingly deferring something even though you expect the delay to make you worse off." We all know when we are procrastinating; it's a familiar feeling of self-conflict with the one side of us that just wants to get it done, and the other side that says why do it now when there's time tomorrow. I think that although the delay may not always make us worse off, if we continue to delay it will eventually make us worse off. It's the degree to which we procrastinate that decides whether we'll be worse off from it. When rationalizing with ourselves, we always tell ourselves that we will have time tomorrow; Surowiecki brings up a good point saying " … we fail to take into account that tomorrow the temptation to put off work will be just as strong." The thing about procrastination is that once you start, it becomes difficult to actually do the work you are procrastinating. As Surowiecki says, we will be just as tempted to procrastinate the next day, and this cycle will continue until we are out of time to procrastinate.

My classmate Bart Phillips has a good deal of experience with procrastinating, he knows what it's like to be [a] student who procrastinates. In a narrative about procrastinating Phillips said, "For me I never felt the need to get work done right away. I always felt like the only way I could work was if I had to." Phillips is agreeing with both sources in this quote because part of the essence of procrastinating is not doing things right away and just putting it off until the last minute. Phillips goes on further saying, "Procrastinating for me is something I wish I didn't do." I think this completely agrees with my other sources and what I've been saying in this essay. When procrastinating we know we shouldn't be doing it but we continue to anyway. As Surowiecki said, procrastination is a strong example of doing something against our better judgment; Phillips shows that this is a common theme among procrastinators.

Procrastinating is something a lot of people do against their better judgment. Graham, Surowiecki, and Phillips all agree that procrastination is a vicious cycle that once started is hard to break. Not wanting to do work and filling your time with other things is a downfall of procrastinators. We recognize in ourselves when we are procrastinating and we also recognize that it is something we shouldn't do because of the possible disadvantage it will give us in doing our work. But still we continue to push things off until the last second, ignoring the consequences and doing the work at the last second possible.

As I'll demonstrate shortly, Darren does a lot of things well here, making the task seem challenging. How did he, to go perhaps the most challenging part of the task, come up with his thesis on student procrastination? It's an abstract problem to which, again, there is a concrete solution: note-taking strategies. As you'll see, Darren discovered his argument for what the essence of being a procrastinating student by finding out what his sources have to say. You can do the same.

I recommend using different note-taking methods with your reflective and descriptive sources. With your reflective sources, I recommend using Behrens and Rosen's method (Chapter 2). It's designed to produce summaries that confirm a source's argument, and it is better suited to working with larger chunks of text (because you use it to find traces of the argument—and that's it). With your descriptive one, the phenomenological themes approach (also Chapter 2) is definitely the one to take. That requires a line-by-line treatment of your classmate's LED, but it means you also (1) always carefully rule out unrelated or redundant material and are (2) focused on finding the essential characteristics that make an experience what it is. But like Darren, you will have to show how the themes of the experience are present not only in your classmate's account but also in your published sources, and that means translating your notes about a source's main points in support of its argument into themes that could apply to other sources that deal with the same experience. I'll call this translating activity *naming themes*, and the tables below can help you both name and organize examples of them into a single place. First, following Behrens and Rosen, you should begin by highlighting or underlining where the text says something that seems important. Write down marginal notes that informally summarize any of these passages or points if you like; they will make your job easier as you move toward identifying the work's argument. Ultimately, you must also divide the work into sections and write descriptions of each in your own language. I include some selected highlights and section descriptions here:

- ▪ "There are three variants of procrastination, depending on what you do instead of working on something: you could work on (a) nothing, (b) something less important, or (c) something more important. That last type, I'd argue is good procrastination" (86)

- ▪ " ... it's easier to get yourself to work on small problems than big ones" (89)

*Section Descriptions*

- ▪ Procrastination = delay of more/less important work
- ▪ Bad kind = working on small problems easily done

## Strategy #3: Create A Table of Possible Themes

With this note-taking done, you can integrate your notes into a table like the the following:

**TABLE 3.6:** Table of Possible Themes

| | Theme 1: Avoiding work by doing something else | Theme 2: Everyone does it | Theme 3: Can be something aligned with purposes | Theme 4: Can be something at odds with purposes | Theme 5: Do less purposeful acts because they are easy |
|---|---|---|---|---|---|
| **Source 1: Graham** | "what you do instead of working on something" (86) | | "something more important" (86) | "something less important" (86) | "it's easier to get yourself to work on small problems than big ones" (89) |
| **Source 2: Surowiecki** | "willingly deferring something" | "temptation … will be just as strong" | | "doing something against one's own better judgment" | |
| **LED** | "I never felt the need to get work done right away" | | | "something I wish I didn't do" | |

Although naming these themes is a back-and-forth process of combining and dividing, using a Table of Possible Themes makes pattern finding not only a matter of *reading* but also *seeing*. To choose the first theme, doing one thing "instead" of another, "deferring," and not feeling "the need" are all related to one another: all signifying "avoidance," they are synonyms. Seeing them stacked invites questions. Is anything essential being lost here? Is "work" getting too much of an emphasis in this theme? The goal for the writer is to entertain these alternatives until she or he starts seeing the same patterns repeat themselves. In the end, Darren emphasized themes 1 and 4 in his analysis, as looking at his thesis here shows:

> We know we have work that needs to be done, but just can't bring ourselves to do it, even though we know we should; that is what being a procrastinator is all about.

It seems Darren's analysis has led him to agree more with Surowiecki and his classmate than with Graham; what we know is that he used note-taking to arrive at his themes, and that the themes he considered most essential are at the heart of his thesis ("avoiding work" and doing something "at odds"). The same note-taking approaches can help you find both your own themes and your argument.

### Strategy #4: Assess Your Use of IMRD Format

Whereas the note-taking approaches can guide your analysis and argument, another strategy uses expectations for how your project must be organized to guide how you draft and revise your project: the Introduction, Methodology, Results, and Discussion (IMRD) format, which most natural and social science-based reports follow. The methodology section is where researchers explain how they gathered and analyzed their data, which for the phenomenological case are both understood (you have one classmate's narrative, and you are reading for themes). In other words, the $M$ is implicit, so I'm leaving it out of this strategy. The rest of the generic structure will be there, though, and that does indeed more than tell you how your project needs to be organized. It also cues you in on questions you can ask yourself to ensure your readers receive the message you mean to send. In your case project, your introduction and theory sections will be your $I$; your "test case," your $R$; and your conclusion, your $D$. Your thesis is going to come at the end of that introduction; for your work to be intelligible to social scientists, it's going to need to, for they expect to not have to read your entire project to know your purpose and findings. In this way, the IMRD structure raises questions you can answer to determine if you've communicated your point effectively. I've listed some of these in Table 3.7.

**TABLE 3.7:** IRD Inventory: Questions to Ask Yourself

| | |
|---|---|
| **Introduction and Theory** (the *I*) | Title<br>■ Does your title make clear what experience you are investigating?<br><br>Hook<br>　■ Do you provide an example that suggests your phenomenon is important?<br>　■ Do you provide an example that demonstrates how there isn't agreement on what your phenomenon is all about?<br><br>Thesis<br>　■ Does your thesis reflect the themes of the experience your sources introduce? Specifically, does it emphasize a source of tension within the experience that draws the themes together while making clear why the experience is worth researching? Does it show how the themes are meaningfully related in the experience?<br><br>Literature Review<br>*Evaluating sources*<br>　■ Do you have at least two professional sources?<br>　■ Do they clearly emphasize your experience?<br>　■ Do they emphasize how there is some agreement upon the essential characteristics of the experience?<br><br>*Identifying themes*<br>　■ Do they emphasize how there is some disagreement upon those characteristics?<br><br>*Concluding the introduction*<br>　■ Do you argue more research on this phenomenon is needed by pointing to these disagreements, how the phenomenon is important, and so on? |
| **Test Case** (the *R*) | Deciding on Your Themes<br>　■ Are your themes repeated enough by your sources that you consider them essential to the experience?<br><br>Presenting Your Themes<br>　■ Do you explicitly name your themes?<br>　■ Do you provide examples from your classmate's narrative of all themes?<br>　■ Do you use your reflection on your classmate's examples to refer to your professional sources? |
| **Conclusion** (the *D*) | ■ Do you recap the thesis's argument?<br>■ Do you explain how your thesis reflects the analysis you have just done?<br>■ Do you explain how it reflects and contributes to research on this phenomenon? |

Again, if we turn to Darren's piece, the generic—that is, IMRD-inspired—quality of his thesis is clear: "We know we have work that needs to be done, but just can't bring ourselves to do it, even though we know we should; that is what being a procrastinator is all about." The second half of his thesis (and the title, "Being a Student Who Procrastinates") names the experience clearly, just as it should. Asking this question—"Does your thesis reflect the themes of the experience your sources introduce?" though, helped him finish the job, in his thesis's second half. Likewise, the values inherent in the IMRD structure—reflected in the IRD Inventory—raises questions you can use to draft and revise your project.

## Strategy #5: Get an LED

The note-taking strategies you use and the IMRD format can keep you focused on persuasively communicating the argument you want to make. But entertainment is also, as everyone knows, about delivering thrills. In addition to being the data source for the next to last section of your paper, the "Test Case," the LED can help you finish your piece with a bang.

Let me say a little about what an LED is and what's involved in writing one. An LED is a description of what it was like for someone else (ideally a classmate) to "live" the experience you're interested in writing on, written by that person. It is a response to the request, "Tell me about a time you [had the experience I'm interested in]." Your classmate should start with the most memorable event he or she can recall, and after that write about ideally two or three other moments that stand out. Generally speaking, an LED should be one to two pages long (250–500 words), and it should take someone 1–1.5 hours to write. An LED does not need to be well organized or well edited, and it should not try to draw all of its examples together into an argument about what the essence of the experience was for its author. The only goal of an LED is a rich description of a few moments in the life of a person, as he or she had the experience.

Let me share an LED with you. One of my students was writing a phenomenological case project on being a student with a job. Because I had worked as a bookseller as an undergraduate student, I offered to write him an LED. Here is an excerpt:

> ### BOX 3.3: MY EXPERIENCE OF BEING A STUDENT WHO HAS A JOB
>
> I only had a job for a small part of my undergraduate experience. At that time, I was between degrees, having completed my BA in history at St. Olaf College and preparing to reapply for graduate programs in English. I had tons of credits,

but I had taken very few literature classes; furthermore, I hadn't studied much for the GRE when I took it the first time. Also, I hadn't had any of my professors review my materials before sending them in. Needless to say, these had all been major oversights.

The best thing to do seemed to be to return to my hometown of Ames, Iowa, and register for classes at Iowa State University. Since I hoped to not live with my parents, I knew I would need a job. So, I decided to apply for what I thought was an appropriate job for an English major: a position as a bookseller at the Waldenbooks store at the mall near my house. I'd be on the job and take in the rarified air of fresh paperbacks. On breaks, I could go to Hardees. It sounded pretty good. Fortunately, the store manager noticed my application. The reason? As I found out at my interview, he had been a friend of my cousin Bill in high school.

So, what was it like to have that job? Well, at the beginning I found it pretty stressful. The most stressful part was learning to use the register. I could see how quick the senior booksellers were at keying in amounts, at conducting searches in the store's database; of course, they needed to look at nothing. Lines would queue up when I was at the controls; I'd tap on the concealed buzzer for reinforcements; a senior bookseller would appear; and the line would dwindle, all while I kept on trying to avoid having to void another transaction or feeling like a swindler by trying to sell another customer on one of the "preferred reader" cards. The worst part, though, of being at the register was the fact that the system kept track of all of the booksellers' data—average transaction time, error frequency counts, and more. These got printed out in the backroom as a kind of incentive. Well, it certainly scared me into trying to be as fast as possible. At first it made me more error prone, but I ultimately found out that my manager didn't really care very much about my speed at the register. What mattered more were human relations skills—which I had down—and being trustworthy, which I also thought I excelled in.

Actually, there were a few moments during the year I worked in the store, though, that my human relations skills seemed worse than I had thought them to be. One time, I recall, a customer was interested in doing a special order of a cookbook of foods from the Balkan peninsula, but he thought it was called the "Baltic" peninsula—which isn't a peninsula at all, and is a region with totally different foods (Greece is at the southernmost tip of the Balkan peninsula; the Baltic states were once part of the Soviet Union. So, we are talking about opposites in so many ways: cold versus hot, canned versus fresh, cabbages versus olives).

> Well, as I entered into a small debate with the customer over what the region's proper name was, I quickly learned the meaning of the phrase "the customer is always right."
>
> As far as trustworthiness goes, while I was occasionally a few minutes late, I never missed a shift, and unlike two other employees, I didn't start pocketing cash from the register. (They were caught.)

You will note a few things: my tone is informal. Also, I let myself get drawn into describing aspects of the job richly (in this case, the stress of the register reports in the backroom, customer conflicts) —a very good thing, because any LED is a response to the statement, "tell me about a time you had [the experience]," a request for description.

Ideally, you will write one of these for a classmate's project.

In your own phenomenological case paper, though, you will make the LED written by someone else the focus of your project's "Test Case" section, where you will

- name themes (using the same ones developed using strategy #1);
- provide examples drawn from the LED of that theme at work in your classmate's experience; and
- reflect on each example for how it (dis)agrees with what your professional sources argue the experience is all about.

Writing about this LED will allow your project to end on an entertaining note. Specifically, it will force you to write about a text by someone you know that has been written about nowhere else. It's one thing to write about a published piece by a stranger; sure, you want to be fair in the points you make, but the feeling that you might add to what's been said about your topic is hard to dodge. You will be responding to works others have published—and others have likely written on—after all. With an LED, you have something to add to what people know about your topic, a story you do not want to get wrong. It's an entertaining opportunity the entire paper builds toward, so go and show how it reflects your themes.

## Two Assignments with Rubrics

I'm going to conclude this chapter as I will the next two with assignment sheets and rubrics designed for possible use with this chapter. The sample papers are responses to these particular tasks. They are printed on separate pages to allow for photocopying.

# RHETORICAL ANALYSIS ASSIGNMENT SHEET

Following some introductory material, I want you to describe the audience and the argument (if possible, the thesis) and provide a summary of a short source on the student experience (article, chapter, advertisement, etc.). Your thesis should focus on this problem: **how does your source persuade its audience to accept its argument?** For the remaining two to three pages, demonstrate how your source persuades its audience, focusing on how it

- notes assumptions held or ignored;

- examines or avoids objections and counterevidence; and

- uses evidence such as definitions, cases, analogies (for example, "choosing a school is like buying a house; one needs to inspect it in person to make a good decision"), authoritative testimony (a respected source is quoted or referred to), or statistics; and

- uses a logos, ethos, and/or pathos, or an informed, ethical, or entertaining (patriotic, humorous, etc.) voice.

Emphasizing one or two of these is enough. If you write on an article or chapter, you may focus on the entire chapter, but you may also concentrate on how a particular section is pivotal in making the chapter (un)persuasive.

# RHETORICAL ANALYSIS RUBRIC

| | A | B | C | D | F |
|---|---|---|---|---|---|
| **Thesis** | Focused thesis identifies topic and sophisticated argument (the writer's position on the source's persuasiveness), possibly previews essay | Identifiable, focused thesis refers to topic, but argument is less sophisticated | General, obvious thesis; argument unclear | General, obvious thesis, if any; lacks discernable argument | No thesis |
| **Support** | Establishes authority through citing, integrating, and interpreting varied source material, including direct quotations that both challenge and support argument. Support must be drawn from how source notes assumptions held, ignored, etc.; examines or avoids objections and counterevidence; uses evidence such as statistics, analogies, etc.; and its use of logos, ethos and/or pathos. Support develops and clarifies writer's argument on source's persuasiveness | Cites and integrates varied source material; interpretation tied to main idea of paragraph, mostly; challenges and supports argument | May use source well in some sections, but argument feels somewhat lost; acknowledges some objections | Superficial use of predictable, unreliable evidence, possibly not drawn from source at all; objections not addressed in a discernable way | No evidence; no source; objections not addressed in a discernable way |
| **Organization** | Topic sentences introduce paragraphs focused on single ideas connected to thesis; transitions within and between paragraphs; intentional organization or plan clear. Topic sentences introduce paragraphs focused on single ideas connected to thesis; transitions within and between paragraphs; intentional organization or plan clear. | Few errors that do not distract | Observes IRD format. Topic sentences don't identify main paragraph ideas or connect with thesis; transitions often missing; multiple or changing plan(s) | Appears to ignore IRD format. Topic sentences and transitions lacking; disorganized | IRD format unrecognizable. No topic sentences, transitions, or discernable plan; fragmented |

| | A | B | C | D | F |
|---|---|---|---|---|---|
| **Mechanics** | Free of errors; none or few mechanical errors | Same as description for A. | Some, repeated errors that occasionally distract | Weak mechanics | Weak mechanics |
| **Publication Style** | Observes correct page format, uses in-text citations to indicate every borrowed idea (either summarized or directly quoted), and includes citations page with entry for selection | | Same as description for A. | Lacking any of features of A. | Lacking all features of A. |

# PHENOMENOLOGICAL CASE ASSIGNMENT SHEET

For this paper of between 750–1000 words (three to four double-spaced pages), you will argue what the essence of a student experience is—what, at its core, a certain experience is "all about." To do so, you will examine how a specific case speaks to professional literature on the same phenomenon. You want to see yourself as writing a thesis-based essay that would appeal to the readership of a college newspaper. Here is what this paper should look like:

1. Following an attention-getting introduction, you want to argue what the essence of this student experience is.
2. Then, as background, you want show how others have described the essence of this experience. You must do by consulting at least two outside sources, ideally ones from Anderson. If you need to go outside of Anderson for your sources, please consult me.
3. Then, you want to test the arguments your sources make about this student experience by examining a case of this experience: an informal, 250–500 word narrative written for you by a classmate. *So, you are not going to be writing about your experience; you are going to be writing about a classmate's.*
4. In the end, you want to conclude by arguing what you take the essence of this student experience to be, considering your sources and your case.

# PHENOMENOLOGICAL CASE RUBRIC

| | A | B | C | D | F |
|---|---|---|---|---|---|
| **Thesis** | Focused thesis identifies topic and sophisticated argument (your position on the essence of your experience), possibly previews essay | Identifiable, focused thesis refers to topic, but argument is less sophisticated | General, obvious thesis; argument unclear | General, obvious thesis, if any; lacks discernable argument | No thesis |
| **Support** | Establishes authority through citing, integrating, and interpreting source material, including direct quotations that both challenge and support argument. | Cites and integrates varied source material; interpretation tied to main idea of paragraph, mostly; challenges and supports argument | May use source well in some sections, but argument feels somewhat lost; acknowledges some objections | Superficial use of predictable, unreliable evidence, possibly not drawn from source at all; objections not addressed in a discernable way | No evidence; no source; objections not addressed in a discernable way |
| **Organization** | Observes IRD format. Also, topic sentences introduce paragraphs focused on single ideas connected to thesis; transitions within and between paragraphs; intentional organization or plan clear | Few errors that do not distract | Observes IRD format. Topic sentences don't identify main paragraph ideas or connect with thesis; transitions often missing; multiple or changing plan(s) | Appears to ignore IRD format. Topic sentences and transitions lacking; disorganized | IRD format unrecognizable. No topic sentences, transitions, or discernable plan; fragmented |
| **Mechanics** | Free of errors; none or few mechanical errors | Same as description for A. | Some, repeated errors that occasionally distract | Weak mechanics | Weak mechanics |
| **Publication Style** | Observes correct page format, uses in-text citations to indicate every borrowed idea (either summarized or directly quoted), and includes citations page with entry for selection | | Same as description for A. | Lacking any of features of A. | Lacking all features of A. |

CHAPTER 4

# BEING A COMMUNITY MEMBER

As I've argued throughout this book, entertaining writing means writing-to-learn about a focused, everyday topic that interests you to the point that your prejudices get challenged and you experience bliss—a transformation in how you think and write that make you a different person from that point forward. As Chapter 3 shows, the experience of schooling is a pathway to everyday topics for entertaining writing. The same is true of the experience of being a community member. As in the schooling chapter, I use Chapter 4, first, to provide you with strategies for finding a focused topic on being a community member; second, to introduce you to two genres you can use to do entertaining writing: the place-based case and the structured revision.

## Another Everyday Topic: Being a Community Member

What is a community? Particular kinds of people—being a reader and writer for that matter—share the same values and beliefs, habits and practices. Because of what they share, those people are a community.

Although communities can be digital (for example, players of a particular MMORPG or subscribers to a particular Twitter account), the focus of this chapter is on physical ones, the limits—the particularities, the *peculiarities*—of which can be exposed and exploited when you write-to-learn.

Today, it is easy to argue that places are losing their local color. Mom and pop stores are closing down as big boxes set up shop. Computers (desktops, laptops, smartphones, and tablets) are everywhere, so everyone must use the same hardware and software to communicate. These similarities are a fact of life. Still, there is a lot of local color out there. If communities were the same, wouldn't you be able to move from one town to another and feel at home immediately? If communities were the same, might not starting up a new relationship be a fairly straightforward matter? The fact is, this place is not that place, however related they may be. That is to say, being a member of any community is always significant—and a source of many intriguing topics for writing.

It can be difficult to perceive that potential, though, when you're standing in one place where life may seem intensely static, inconsequential yet all-encompassing: being an adolescent in your hometown. For me, that meant Ames, Iowa, in the 1980s. When I wasn't doing my homework, sitting in a study hall reading *National Geographic*, riding around in my friend's station wagon (an olive-green Vista Cruiser we called the "Zepmobile"), eating a microwave-heated ("nuked") hot dog, or sleeping, you might have found me hitting a tennis ball against the inside of my parents' garage, thinking about the massive skyscrapers I hoped to build one day in my hometown to rescue it (and me) from obscurity. When I look at the list behind me, I see a lot of period- and place-specific detail (no computer access in study hall, for example), but back then, I felt like a featureless speck of dust. Now, as a white, middle-class male, I certainly had many advantages (among them, a steady supply of hot dogs), but I didn't know what many of them were. Wasn't my town, well, normal? That's what I thought, for experience had exposed me to little else, and—as I discussed in the last chapter—the formal learning rarely took the location of my schools as a subject.

## Inventories for Researching Being a Community Member

With a little research, though, I could have seen a lot more. As much as I had felt far away from centers of power in my hometown, my experience of being a community member in Ames was not so particular to have no relation to life elsewhere.

If I use another inventory to link my activities to the social institutions they are associated with, these broader ties become easy to see:

---

**TABLE 4.1:** Inventory #1: Activities, Institutions, and Roles

| Activity | Associated Institution (and roles you perform within each) |
| --- | --- |
| **Doing homework** | School (student in required and elective courses, college-track student, etc.), government (as citizen, legal subject, cultural actor; future taxpayer; etc.), economy (TV-, book-, magazine-, newspaper-, paper-, pencil/pen-user; clothing-wearer; current unskilled and future (un)skilled worker); family (middle-class student of college educated-parents; Protestant child (embodying "work ethic" where one labors to reveal evidence of being among the "elect"[1]); younger, unathletic sibling of former varsity athlete brother currently enrolled in college; son of former music teacher in district junior high school; etc.) |
| **Being in a study hall** | School, government, cohort (this basically means the people you went to school with; so, roles played in this setting include the following: friend, teammate, neighborhood resident, classmate—in geometry, earth science, etc.), economy, etc. |
| **Driving around with friends** | Cohort, government, economy (fast-food customer, gasoline-user, etc.) |

1  *See description of Protestant work ethic, a term coined by Max Weber, https://en.wikipedia.org/wiki/Protestant_work_ethic.*

---

It took me a while to identify these roles, but with an institution named, roles kept appearing. Everyday actions are part of community life, as mundane as they may seem, and once you name them, potential topics for writing show up (such as being a student who eats at fast-food restaurants). The trick is connecting these activities "up"—to typical behaviors in a community, to a community's cultural institutions, or to larger political and economic forces that shape a community's life. The above inventory can start you on your way.

## Inventory #2: Inside Scoop

Another inventory, which I'll call "Inside Scoop," can help in a similar way. You must begin with a scenario: Imagine a person is going to visit a community you know well for a day and wants to have a taste of what makes the town the type of place it is. Provide a list of activities and explain why these reveal the town's essence. Here is how I would fill this inventory out for the city I live in, Plattsburgh, New York.

**TABLE 4.2:** Inside Scoop

| Place | Reason |
|---|---|
| The municipal beach or Cumberland Head State Park | Plattsburgh is on the shores of Lake Champlain, a 120-mile-long freshwater lake. It also happens to have beautiful beaches, which are best in the summer but offer great views year round. The Champlain Valley is also a microclimate and the lake a home to a lot of commerce. So, one can't understand Plattsburgh without coming to terms with the lake. |
| Livingoods, Plattsburgh Brewing Company | The Champlain Valley is also an agricultural region, and because of Plattsburgh's proximity to "locavore," crunchy Vermont, locally grown food is pretty easy to come by here. All of these restaurants serve it. |
| Rockwell Kent Gallery, Nina Winkel Sculpture Gallery, Samuel de Champlain Monument, etc. | Good, free art is pretty easy to come by in Plattsburgh. These two galleries, both located at SUNY Plattsburgh, are good examples. The Kent is bigger and reveals more about area history. The colonialism-celebrating Champlain monument is public art located in the most beautiful spot in the city (https://www.flickr.com/photos/new-yorkled/4772287274). |

My own interests in food come across here; another Plattsburgher would give you a different list. Still, the defense of my choices in the right-hand column allows me to connect these places "up"—to see them as important parts of my community's life. How "good, free art" is easy to find in Plattsburgh is interesting, given that people pay to see art the world over (museum fees, concert tickets, etc.). A number of topics on being a community member come into view—installations of particular works (http://www.wptz.com/news/artists-create-new-mural-in-downtown-plattsburgh/35061422); Nina Winkel's decision to give much of her sculpture to SUNY Plattsburgh; and the role of one arts organization, the North Country Cultural Center, in the community for the arts come to mind. Other topics related to hockey (what does it mean to be a SUNY Plattsburgh women's hockey team member?) or food (the rise of the Blue Collar Bistro (Levit, 2014) from farmer's market kiosk to full-fledged restaurant as evidence of a growing "locavore" culture in Plattsburgh) also come to mind.

### Inventory #3: Different Strokes

Here is another related inventory. Picture at least two people (one of whom may be yourself) who live in a community, and using set categories (place to have lunch, greatest social problem, etc.), have each give his/her best answer to each category, explaining why he or she would make this choice above all others.

**TABLE 4.3:** Inventory #3: Different Strokes

|  | Person #1 | Person #2 |
|---|---|---|
| Best place to have lunch | | |
| Favorite local publication | | |
| Most important student club | | |

I've described this as a role-playing opportunity, but you could also use this table to get responses from classmates, friends, and others.

### Inventory #4: Town Self-Image

This is another useful for tool for drawing a community's identity—its theory of itself—into view. Turn to traditional institutions within one town or city, and you will begin to see other events or places within that municipality that send a message about what life is like there. The following table can guide you.

| Artifact | Screen Shot (with at least two examples—events, places, activities, organizations, etc.—of life in this place) | Reflection (What do two examples of life in this place suggest the town's self-image is?) |
|---|---|---|
| **Major town newspaper (look for lists of major news stories on its homepage, lists of area events, etc.)** | <br>Source: The Press-Republican. | Plattsburgh's newspaper, *The Press-Republican*, brought me to this list. I note two things of importance: more free public art ("Peter Russom Art Exhibit" and "Trombone Rapture") and a series of events hosted by a nearby ski resort, Jay Peak. Public art and skiing: Those are two meaningful aspects of life in my city. Because I'm already interested in free public art, I'm thinking I could have a potential topic: What does the Plattsburgh State Art Museum say about the culture of Plattsburgh? |
| **Town Wikipedia page** | | |
| **Church website** | | |
| **High school yearbook (table of contents, major clubs, etc.)** | | |

Creating a screen shot is easy (on a PC, it's Ctrl-Alt-Print Screen; on an Apple, it's ⌘-shift-3). Once you have made these key strokes, tap on the correct table box, hit "paste," and you'll see your screen shot. If you'd care to crop the image, you can do that easily with photoediting software, such as Photoshop or GIMP (https://www.gimp.org/downloads/), the latter of which is free. Returning to the table, though, this is a low-stakes opportunity to collect and compare documents and items they include. A "Town's Self-Image" table is, then, a way to set aside at least some of your prejudices about life in a place and look for themes that say, "life is like this here."

Each inventory reveals the same thing: being a community member is something you do every day that is social, meaningful, and researchable.

The key is focusing on some aspect of institutionalized life—a specific event (a parade, the firing of a teacher thought to be "too liberal" or "too conservative," etc.) or place (a café, a monument, etc.)—about which you can ask: how does this event or place reflect this community's culture?

## Beyond Inventories: Social Theory and Public Data to the Rescue

Let's hang onto that question. The importance of identifying an event or place in a community's life that is meaningful to you can't be understated; you will not be able to write-to-entertain on this topic without it. Still, your task is to argue how that event or place reflects a community's *culture*. Culture is such a big idea, it's hard to say anything meaningful about it without consulting sources. There's a good reason for this that is captured by a recent term for describing how community cultures and outside forces link up: the "glocal." Here is one definition of "glocal": "the simultaneity—the co-presence—of both universalizing and particularizing tendencies" ("Glocalization," *Wikipedia*). An example the Wikipedia page this is drawn from cites is the McDonald's restaurant. Every McDonald's location comes from elsewhere and can kill local competition, undercut farm-to-table relationships, and more. At the same time, local favorites (such as beer in a German McDonald's, a croissant at a Quebecois one, etc.) find their way onto the menu. Each McDonald's restaurant is not the same. Rather, each McDonald's restaurant combines global and local forces in one place—each pushing on the other. So, why does consulting sources allow you to say something meaningful about life in a place? The two are related, of course. How do you begin to see the "glocal" flavor of an event, place, or person in a community? Two such sources are social theories and public data.

To return to an earlier example, my hometown of Ames, Iowa, seemed to me a pretty average place as a kid. Was my life in my city, then, indistinguishable from life in other places? You may recall my family and I attended a conservative Lutheran church at the time. In attending that church, were we being particularly "Ames-ish"? If you had asked high school me that question on the street, I might have said "sort of." Had I sat down to write-to-learn in response to that question, though, armed with accessible social theory and public data, I would have been able discover I had an interesting topic on my hands.

Let's say I had, then, turned to a nonfiction book I have asked hundreds of eighteen-year-olds to read: Bill Bishop's *The Big Sort*. Some other readable social theory books that would serve equally well for a place-based case include the following:

1. Charles Murray's *Coming Apart*
2. Robert Putnam's *Bowling Alone*
3. Nick Reding's *Methland*
4. Thandeka's *Learning to Be White*
5. Colin Woodard's *American Nations*

To continue with my example, though, Bill Bishop argues post–World War II affluence has led Americans to politically segregate into communities that reflect certain lifestyle "choice[s]" (Bishop, 39). He explains the concept of politically segregated communities in an interview with Mike Shea for *Texas Monthly*:

> [O]pposites do not attract. We talk about assortative mating when it comes to marriage. People tend to mate with those like themselves. … What we're talking about here is a society-wide case of assortative mating when it comes to how and where we live. We are finding comfort around those who share our interests—religion, sports, Internet sites, lifestyles, politics. Like does attract like. But, as you say, there is a power in people trying to avoid those who are different. Certainly, God help those who find themselves living in places where they are in the minority. Political scientists have known for half a century that political minorities vote less—political minorities are even less likely to participate in civic activities.
>
> In my deeply Democratic neighborhood (Travis Heights in Austin), a Republican once ventured on to the Internet news group and was not so politely told to find someplace else to live. In one deeply Republican Hill Country town, Democrats built a July 4th float, but when it came time for the parade, nobody would ride. Nobody wanted to be publicly identified as a Democrat. Luckily, it rained and so the Ds were spared the ignominy of having a riderless float.

Such communities as Travis Heights and the unnamed Hill Country town are ones where people with "share[d] … interests"—including political beliefs—are increasingly moving. Bishop is not arguing this is a good thing, as his points about the silencing of minorities suggest. Still, Bishop's argument is national in scope; that means it can be related to—and tested against—life in any American town, including my hometown. If I had had access to his book as an eighteen-year-old, Bishop would have given me the ability to state this: there might be an Ames lifestyle reflected in its residents' politics. Looking around my church, I would have seen a lot of white people. In terms of a lifestyle, that wouldn't have been very descriptive. If I'd have looked beyond my church's walls, though, I would have been able to list qualities of my town that made it unlike neighboring cities. It had a lot of students (about 30,000 of them in 2015) and veterinarians (the National Veterinary Services Laboratory was founded there in 1961). It also had an upscale, "New York-style" bistro, Aunt Maude's, which remains popular today (think disposable income—and really good French onion soup). Considering Bishop's idea of a city "lifestyle" and looking around a bit, I could have seen more than race but, also, class (specifically, middle class, college-educated people). With Bishop, I could have seen Ames had a lifestyle.

Was being a member of my church a reflection of the town's lifestyle? I might have hit a wall here, given that my family was a match for the lifestyle so far. In Bishop's terms, I would probably have assumed I had a case of "assortative mating" on my hands. To link the town's politics to its lifestyle, I would have had to look further, going to a site like Dave Leip's *Atlas of US Presidential Elections* (2012). If you are from a community in America, you will find how your county has voted in U.S. presidential elections since 1960 in a matter of seconds. Leip's site suggests my hometown typically votes Democratic, as his visuals on the returns for the 2004 and 2008 presidential elections show:

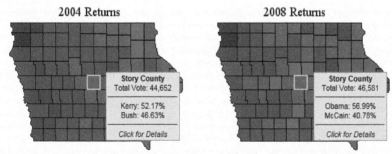

FIGURE 4.1: Press Republican Events  Source: Dave Leip's Atlas of U.S. Presidential Elections.

Although my county does not lean heavily toward one party, these data would have left me wondering if I was a little less normal for my area than I had once thought. That is, was I a conservative youth in a liberal town?

I might have asked, "Am I—or am I not—a reflection of my hometown's lifestyle? I satisfy a lot of the categories, but I go to St. Paul's. Where does that fit in?" St. Paul's belonged then and today to the Lutheran Church Missouri Synod (LCMS), in which the highest-profile leadership roles (pastors, elders, public readers of scripture, etc.) are typically reserved for males. St. Paul's was then and is today a conservative church, but in looking for traces of the Ames lifestyle under its roof, I might have found a number of things:

1. Female ushers and scripture readers
2. A liberal communion policy (if you were an adult, they didn't require you to present your paperwork; the visiting adult "believer" was welcome)
3. Fair-trade, shade-grown organic coffee for sale in the fellowship hall (a thing the post-2000 me would have found)

Was St. Paul's a relatively progressive LCMS congregation? I would have known it was possible at that moment. This might have rattled me, intrigued me, been something I'd want to disprove with other counterevidence—and, then again, it might have been a chance to see my congregation was a part of something much bigger than itself, a feature of a grand political and cultural landscape.

This is all to say that armed with an inventory, social theory, and public data, I could have unmoored myself from the idea that nothing of note was happening in Ames. I would have had an example of life in a community I cared about I could use to test the predictions of others. It would have been a powerful thought. It would have been a chance to do entertaining writing—to write to celebrate and refine what I valued, the same thing you can do right now by writing-to-learn on the topic of being a community member.

If you're at a loss on where to start, consider doing an inventory right now. If it also helps you, here is a list of possible topics I have given my students in the past:

1. How was Walmart able to open a store in Williston, VT?
2. Is Burlington, VT, a mecca for liberals?
3. How did a Ten Commandments monument get erected on the grounds of the Haskell County, OK, courthouse?
4. Does First Bible Church in Staten Island, NY, reflect the borough's politics?
5. Who founded SUNY Plattsburgh's Environmental Action Committee? Who belongs to it now?

6. Why does one conservative church in Ames, IA, have a liberal communion policy?

7. Why is the town of Bridgewater the only remaining "dry" town in the state of Connecticut?

## Genre #1: Place-Based Case

As in Chapter 3, I want to introduce a couple of genres here, focusing on the tools they offer you to keep writing entertaining from start to finish. As with other genres, there is no substitute for a commitment to your topic. The closer to the ground, to everyday experience, your topic gets, the better; if you are investigating how people are increasingly gravitating to your hometown to live a "granola" lifestyle, the establishment of a local restaurant or band is probably going to be a better topic than the election of a liberal mayor. People vote for mayors, but they inhabit public spaces, tasting menu items and handing over $5 to leave a concert with the band's limited release. There are more surprises, opportunities to be an authority, with everyday topics, as the model essay I'll discuss in this section shows.

But first, let me introduce the genre: the place-based case. Like the phenomenological case, the place-based case asks you to study a single instance of a phenomenon. Whereas the phenomenological case asks you to study a single person's experience, the place-based case asks you to study how a single community's culture is reflected by a particular event or institution (a community theater production, a yacht club, etc.). That reflection is always there, for as organizational theorist John Van Maanen (2011) puts it, culture refers to "how things get done by people on the ground in … [particular] social worlds"—or how life in a place defines particular "words, ideas, things, symbols, groups, identities, activities, and so forth" (154–155). Although I encourage you to study your hometown, it's not essential; if you do, though, you'll be writing about a place that is meaningful to you. You'll also be challenging your prejudices, using both the perspectives of library research and community "natives" to go beyond what you already know about life in that place.

The place-based case also has a generic structure similar to the phenomenological case: It includes an

*Introduction*

■ Lead that possibly provides an example of the experience of concern to create interest in the case.

■ Thesis that argues how a community example (dis)confirms a social theory.

*Theory*

- Here you want to introduce at least one source that presents a social theory for why a community's culture is a particular way. When I teach the place-based case, I typically select this text myself. You will want to summarize its argument. You will also want to introduce, define, and provide borrowed or invented examples of categories important to your analysis.

*Background*

- Here you want to provide some general evidence on the community of interest and possibly the topic. Here public data can be particularly valuable.

*Test Case*

- Here, you want to draw on varied evidence regarding the topic, the aspect of a community's life you are using to test whether a social theory is or is not validated in this place. Quotations from "natives" are essential here. A multimodal set of sources is valuable, too, reflecting contemporary experience and suggesting you have done a thorough job. It is essential you refer to the categories identified in your "theory" section—at least some of which must be drawn from your core published source. Counterarguments are essential, strengthening your character.

*Conclusion*

- Return to your thesis, with the focus being on what we now know about the social theory based on your study of life in one community.

As you can see, the place-based case is like its phenomenological counterpart a theory-testing activity. This is particularly evident in the sample paper I'd like to include now.

### IS CLIFTON PARK, NY A POST-MATERIALISTIC TOWN?

While driving down the streets of the quiet suburban town of Clifton Park, NY, it is hard to believe that during the night, swarms of people flock to the local music venue to listen to bands performing metal, hardcore, and punk music. It is also hard to believe that protests are happening just twenty minutes away in bigger towns such as Albany and Saratoga. Clifton Park seems to be undergoing change. During the 1950s and 1960s, there was a cultural shift going on in America. Citizens were becoming more and more polarized in their culture as well as with their politics. Bill Bishop, author of *The Big Sort* points out dropping church attendance rates, decreasing trust in the government and an increased need for self-expression during this time. Bishop describes this new trend of individuals as "post-materialists." These post-materialists are concerned less about physiological needs and more about self-expression. According to Bishop's description of post-materialistic individuals, Clifton Park could be seen as both materialistic and post-materialistic due to the music scene, politics, economy, and church attendance.

Abraham Maslow, a psychologist known for creating the hierarchy of needs theory, puts physiological needs at the bottom of the hierarchy followed by safety, love, esteem, and finally self-actualization. Ronald Inglehart from the University of Michigan created a hypothesis based of Maslow's theory proposing that "People who knew that their basic needs were satisfied would gradually adopt different values from those who live in scarcity" and "those who grew up in abundance would be more concerned with self-expression" (Bishop 2008, 84). Since Bishop defines prosperity as being able to satisfy basic needs, those who did not have to worry about when or how they will get their next meal, would go on to seek other issues. These individuals are more interested in the environment and human rights issues such as gay rights and abortion. Also, they tend to have a higher degree in education. Materialists are said to be concerned about economic growth, ability to feed family, and military security.

The politics in Clifton Park seem to neither prove nor disprove that Clifton Park is post-materialistic. In Bishop's book, he explains that there is a sorting of neighborhoods and towns into groups that seem to have the same values and political party, however, according to *the US Election Atlas*, 50.8% of Saratoga County voted Democratic for Barack Obama in 2008 and 47.45% voted Republican for John McCain. In 2010, 53.18% voted for Democrat Andrew

Cuomo and 39.93% voted for Republican Carl Paladino for governor (Leip 2012). Both of these elections are pretty close as the breakdown of Democrats to Republicans. Bishop describes post-materialists as being "cultural creative" and tending to have a Democratic lifestyle. But, there have not been any large political sit-ins or protests in Clifton Park that are expected of these post-materialists.

Unlike Clifton Park, twenty minutes away in Albany; there are many actions taken that make Albany's residents seem like they trust traditional institutions and the government. Recently, there was a sit in to protest budget cuts to UAlbany, where students walked out of classes to meet in a quad and protest. Through this protest, they expressed their need for change and hopefulness that Andrew Cuomo will deliver. Also, there are many lobbyists in Albany supporting opposing an array of issues, such as the SUNY budget cuts and redistricting. Another example of Albany trusting the government is unions. There are many labor and teachers unions operating out of Albany. Even from a close distance, two different towns can have different values.

A factor that seems to support Clifton Park's Republican lifestyle rather than the cultural creative lifestyle of the Democrats is church attendance rates. There are 33 places of worship in the 50.2 square miles of Clifton Park. In fact, there is a church right next to Northern Lights and right next to my house. The church next to my house, North Star Church (which is renovated from an old SAAB dealership) is actually geared toward the younger generation it seems. Most of the sermon is a band playing and there are large TVs around the room projecting images of prayer and the band.

Surely from an economic and educational stand point, Clifton Park would seem to fall under the post-materialistic category with a higher median income than the New York average. In 2009, the estimated median household income for Clifton Park was $75,837 while the overall median for New York was much less at $54,659 (City Data 2018). Higher educational attainment can lead to a better job that will lead to higher pay, which would explain why Clifton Park's average income is higher. 27.6% of people in Clifton Park have earned a Bachelor's degree compared to the 15.6% New York average; 13.2% have earned a Master's degree compared to the 8% New York Average (City Data 2018). According to those numbers, one could safely say that Clifton Park, in comparison to some other towns in New York, at a higher monetary advantage. With this monetary success, this could lead to pressures to succeed in school for the children of the parents who are highly educated. In 2009, Shenendehowa Central School District, located in Clifton Park had a graduation rate of 89% and a dropout rate of 5% compared to the New York 74% graduation rate average (*All Over Albany* 2010).

An exceptional example to support the Democratic lifestyle in Clifton Park is its music venue. Although Clifton Park may be seen as a quiet, clean-cut town, a writer from the *New York Times* says that "the richer the town, the more unholy must be the title of the band it spawns (*New York Times*). Clifton Park which houses the music venue, Northern Lights, is no exception to this rule. Northern Lights tends to book very specific genres of music. In an advertisement for an upcoming show, *The Times Union* states, "When heavy metal come to Northern Lights, as it very often does, it comes in great gulps. Sunday, the club hosts an early bill with six bands all trying to out loud each other while the mosh pit whirls (*Times Union*)." Of the fifteen bands booked in the next four months, seven of the bands are some genre of metal; two are posthard-core, two are rock; another two are ska-punk and two others (Northern Lights). In the past, the venue has booked several other ska and punk bands, such as Anti-Flag, Star Fucking Hipsters, and Big D and the Kids Table. These bands sing of post-materialistic values such as the right to choose, war, and human rights. For example, in the song, "A New Kind of Army," Anti-Flag sings: "I'd rather fight to spread some tolerance and unity/ than buy into their nationalistic brainwashing/ killing mothers, fathers, sisters, brothers /common human beings." Also, in the song "Church & Rape" by Star Fucking Hipsters, they address the issue of abortion laws and how they believe that church and state are not completely separated: "Laws dictate these violations when church is state/ the twisted legislation seals every fate/ some just choose suicide to hide their shame/ while in back-alleys most die in pain." Ironically, the small venue is located in a strip mall right in between a dollar store and a church.

Not only is the music itself in Clifton Park a testament to post-materialism, the act of actually being in the crowd is also. On Maslow's hierarchy of needs, love and belongingness needs are third highest on the ladder. In essence, humans have a desire to belong to groups and to be needed. At a show, formal social barriers seem to be broken down. Personal space becomes the space of the group as a whole; strangers jump, sweat, and sometimes bleed on each other and dance with each other. From personal experience, while watching dancer swing their limbs and push into each other in the mosh pit, if someone falls down, almost always someone will stop to help them up. There is even a group named the 518 Wrecking Crew who go to shows for the mosh pits.

Bill Bishop describes post-materialists as educated and financially well-off individuals who are concerned with self-expression. Clifton Park's inhabitants have a higher degree of education and income than the New York average as well as a music scene that addresses issues of self-expression such as abortion laws, war, and the environment. Music in itself is also a form of self-expression. However, Bishop's idea that post-materialists do not have high church attendance rates and have a high rate of sit-ins and protests seem to be disproven by Clifton Park. Overall, Clifton Park does seem to have several post-materialistic values to it, but there are also values that, according to Bishop's ideas, disprove it.

You can see the generic features are here. The theory and background sections, as expected, incorporate social theory (including a summary of Bishop's argument and definitions and examples of key concepts) and public data (Leip's voting data). More importantly, she takes up the theory-testing task effectively. A place-based case should pulse with life, with local color, and it must connect that local case with the social theory at issue. Meghan's description of Northern Lights is rich—and it nicely reflects Bishop's idea of post-materialist "self-expression."

### Strategies #1 and #2: Use Note-Taking Strategies and a Topic Evaluation Table to Arrive at a Focused Topic

Doing entertaining writing always requires a topic you and others care about which you know something but want to know more. Meghan has a great *topic*: her hometown's live music venue as a reflection of that city's lifestyle. Where can you find a topic like this? The inventories above are a good starting point, a chance (1) to decide on a community and (2) to begin asking what life in this place is "all about." That second opportunity that an inventory provides, though, is hard to exploit because culture is difficult to theorize or define.

### Note-Taking Strategies

Again, this is where social theory comes to the rescue. With a source like Bishop by your side, your task becomes concrete: you must, first, understand another person's message. To build this understanding, you can use a note-taking strategy designed to identify its argument. Any of those described in Chapter 2 will do, but I suggest using Behrens and Rosen's approach as it creates useful material for drafting a summary (your "theory" section). Their summary-based note-taking approach, again, asks you to do the following:

1. Read a chapter, identifying words that get explained/defined by the author, examples that stick with you, and so on, that appear to reflect your hunches or predictions for a chapter's argument.
2. Divide the chapter into sections.
3. Write an informal ten word marginal summary to describe each section.
4. Review your marginal summaries, and—then—at the start or end of the chapter, write a version of the chapter's argument.

Doing this on the first few chapters in the book will probably suffice. If you do this, you will have a rich resource for (1) identifying your source's main argument and (2) identifying key terms/concepts you may use to investigate life in your community of interest. If you look at Meghan's first three paragraphs, you'll see she provides her summary of her main source, Bishop's *The Big Sort*, there. I suggest her view of his argument can be seen in two excerpts from her piece:

> Bill Bishop, author of The Big Sort points out [abundance led to] dropping church attendance rates, decreasing trust in the government, and an increased need for self-expression during this time. ... In Bishop's book, he explains that there is a sorting of neighborhoods and towns into groups that seem to have the same values and political party.

If you look at her sense of Bishop's argument here, you'll see a few phrases that "boil down" some part his message: "post-materialist," "abundance," and "self-expression" are three. Your notes can give you similar clues about what your source argues and what its testable key terms or concepts might be.

*Topic Evaluation Table*

Your second step is to test your source's conclusions against a case. But what do you do if you're struggling to find a case, and you're unsure how it might reflect or challenge your source's claims about American life? Using a Topic Evaluation Table can help you answer both questions. You should start out by adding testable key terms or concepts that reflect your source's argument to the column on the table's far left-hand side. Then, you can try out potential topics drawn from an inventory you've completed or elsewhere by identifying them at the top of the remaining columns; then, you should write informally about how any of your source's themes may be reflected in a possible case. The following table is how Meghan might have filled one out for her piece.

TABLE 4.5: Topic Evaluation Table
**Community: Clifton Park**

| Theme from Social Theory Source | Possible Topic #1: School Mascot Change | Possible Topic #2: Northern Lights | Possible Topic #3: ??? |
|---|---|---|---|
| **Post-materi-alism** | | Are people in my hometown liberals or conservatives? I know NY is a "blue state." I should look up the voting returns. | |
| **Abundance** | Was the Shenende-howa School District mascot controversy a sign of wealth? | Seeing live music is expensive—definitely something somebody does when her/his "ba-sic needs" are met. | |
| **Self-expres-sion** | | What acts play there? Their ideas = some reflection of what Clifton Park residents value (like Inglehart's "human rights" supporters?)  Mosh pit: helping people out—that's "human rights" for sure. | |

As I said earlier, when you are writing a place-based case, you are asking, "how does this event or place reflect this community's culture?" If we look at Meghan's example, this question becomes: How does Northern Lights as an alternative live music club reflect the post-materialist, left-leaning, "self-expression" valuing culture of Clifton Park, New York? Using Bishop's keywords has put her in a much different place. You can use the same strategy to arrive at your ideal case.

*Strategies #3 and #4: Use More Tables to Test a Theory Against Your Case.*

Having identified an entertaining topic, it's time to find multiple artifacts that will be your evidence as you describe your community's background and test if your source's social theory describes your case well. This will be the part of your paper that readers will be most interested in getting to because it is the part where you're making a real contribution to the known. Why? Well, in this part of the project, you're either (1) providing additional evidence or clarification for a theory with valuable explanatory power or (2) showing that that theory is flawed.

Your main problem at this point is that you are at risk of failing to entertain the artifacts you find—and how they reflect or challenge your major source's themes. In this sense, I'll point back to the two-halved quality of entertaining: it means to bring something so close that you start to see it differently, and only then to report on what you found. So, it's time to temporarily turn away from the theory and focus exclusively, informally, on what's going on in your community of interest. Because it interests you, ask yourself, "what artifacts in this community pertain to my topic and interest me?" It's time to find and describe them—something like shopping for stuff you like and describing what it is about it you like. This is the time to go small to go big, to praise what makes a thing itself because it's awesome, which no one else may know, so you have to give it now or it will not be given. It is a time for celebrating pieces of evidence as crazy cupcakes.

*Artifacts Table*

One way of doing this is to create an artifacts table, a collection of objects of the value of which you must explain. In the first row, I'd start off by citing public data—voting returns, racial breakdowns, median incomes, etc. For voting returns, I've already mentioned Dave Leip's site, but a lot of community data can be found by visiting the City-Data.com site for the town you are researching. For the following rows, the idea is to get several texts in various media, and although some of these texts can be about your community in general, most should be specifically about your event or setting. If you look at the table below, you'll see how Meghan might have filled it out for her piece.

**TABLE 4.6:** Artifacts Table

| | Summarize, directly quote from, or include (portion of) image. You may want to look for particular categories, but don't use your main source's at this point. | Reflect on what this source says your event or setting—and, generally, the community in which it is located—is "all about." |
|---|---|---|
| Public data | Median household income for Clifton Park was $75,837 (City-Data.com) | Clifton Park is pretty well-off (relative to rest of NY). |
| | In 2008, 50.8% of Saratoga county for Obama, 47.45% for McCain (Leip) | That seems like sort of a slim advantage for the Democrats in Saratoga. I wonder how big that is? Is it purple—and if so, would that rule out Bishop's argument that people have "sorted"? |
| Community artifact #1 | North Star Church | I've been here—it might look conservative (as a church), but the services are contemporary. Seems kind of post-materialist. |
| Community artifact #2 | Northern Lights website | |
| Community artifact #3 | UAlbany protests (*Albany Times-Union*) | Is that trusting government or—as a protests—distrusting it (in a Big Sort-ish, self-expressive way)? |
| | Whirling "mosh pit" at Northern Lights (*Albany Times-Union*) | Self-expression all the way! |
| Community artifact #4 | "twisted legislation" (Star Fucking Hipsters' song) | Reflects interest in/belief in "self-expression"—and how government can't be counted on to serve people's interests well |

I would like to emphasize a few things here. First, you can begin to see how multiple types of evidence emphasize the same themes here (self-expression). That is fodder for creating coherent paragraphs and transitions in an essay—not to mention suggesting language that could be at the heart of a quality thesis. Second, with the public data portion, you are in a low-stakes way responding to what another author has written, which keeps you doing entertaining writing. Third, you can see where there are some missed opportunities in terms of evidence here. More evidence about the North Star Church would be useful; Meghan is relying on some source in the section in her paper about this institution, but we don't know what it is. What about the church's website, a service program, and so on? Another thing I note is that there are no images, videos, or other visual elements here, and that means modalities—opportunities for making really persuasive arguments—are being missed. My point is that an artifact table is a low-stakes place for inventing arguments and analyzing evidence—and, possibly, drafting parts of your piece and speculating how you might effectively organize them (keep North Star Church in one paragraph, end with Northern Lights, etc.).

*Themes and Evidence Table*

You'll note in how I modeled use of the artifacts table, too, that it was difficult for me to block out any references to Bishop, and I think you'll find the same will be true for you. I don't want your theory to taint your analysis, but at some point, you must also come to terms with it. At some point, you must do that explicitly, and the last strategy I'll introduce here—the themes and evidence table—is an opportunity to do that in such a way that you keep on questioning whether you are shortchanging what's really happening in your community of interest. Here is that table, with one of Meghan's themes included for demonstration.

TABLE 4.7: Themes and Evidence Table

| Theme from Social Theory | Community Evidence | Community Counterevidence |
| --- | --- | --- |
| Liberal "self-expression" | Mosh pit | North Star Church |
| | | |
| | | |
| | | |

This is obviously where you fuse what you have gleaned from social theory, public data, and your artifacts. It's, again, a low-stakes space for testing theory—but it is also a place to begin reporting on your findings and, hopefully, drafting material you can integrate into the "test case" section of your place-based case.

## Genre #2: Structured Revision

Being a community member means participating in its culture. To cite Van Maanen (2011) again, culture refers to "how things get done by people on the ground in … [particular] social worlds"—or how life in a place defines particular "words, ideas, things, symbols, groups, identities, activities, and so forth" (154-155). Two important aspects of culture stand out for me here: how a community or group's culture is reflected in (1) shared values that (2) members actions' reflect and, possibly, revise. Your community of interest, like my Ames or Meghan's Clifton Park, may embody these properties, and so must a classroom where entertaining writing is the expectation. This is to draw attention to the fact that classrooms often aren't communities. Many aren't, and the idea that education need only prepare students for the future is a big part of it. (That is, if it sucks today, who cares? It's like medicine that tastes bad but can make you better in time.) Prejudice-challenging, entertaining writing-to-learn is the use of "words," the "activity" at the heart of the composition class that's a community. To the prejudice-challenging part: it is a bacon-and-cheddar cupcake, familiarity with a twist, a transformative act that leaves you bigger and broader forever. I also noted we might call this "serious play," a dynamic oneness with one's subject matter that leaves the player different in the end. There is nothing solitary in this "serious play." It is social interaction, community, as the great John Dewey again demonstrates. To make this point, Dewey (1963) describes what children do at recess:

> Children at recess or after school play games. … [For each game,] the rules are part of the game. They are not outside of it. … As long as the game goes on with a reasonable smoothness, the players do not feel that they are submitting to external imposition but that they are playing the game. … Usually a group of youngsters change the rules by which they play only when the adult group to which they look for models have themselves made a change in the rules, while the change made by elders is at least supposed to conduce to making the game more skillful or more interesting to spectators (52–53).

Playing a game demonstrates how following your bliss, or respecting your purposes, does not mean going rogue but valuing—and, if need be, adding to—the rules. And you are not alone: the rules you play by and possibly add to (to, ideally, make "the game more skillful or more interesting") come from somewhere, from other people—so you are a gamer among gamers, a community member.

Here are the rules of the game when it comes to the structured revision: for this task, you will focus most of your revisions on your use of higher-order criteria, such as thesis, support, and so on—everything except for assignment requirements, MLA style, and mechanics. I ask that structured revisions also include the following sections:

*Cover Letter*

At the beginning of your revised paper, include an at least 250-word cover letter that describes how you sought to improve your paper by revising to exploit its strengths and address its weaknesses in satisfying its criteria, paying greatest attention to higher-order ones.

*Revised Paper*

While the sequence of sections (introduction, theory, etc.) will depend on what kind of piece you are revising (rhetorical analysis, place-based case, etc.), another "section" is the annotations you should make to your piece while having a word processing program's reviewing feature (the "suggesting" feature on Google docs, "track changes" in Word, etc.) turned on the whole time. You should annotate in three ways:

1. First, highlight all changes you make to your revised paper.
2. Second, if you decide to reorganize anything—whether you cut and paste or select, drag, and drop sections elsewhere—be sure a struck-through version remains afterward in your moved sections' original spots. This lets your readers know you have moved text rather than written something new.
3. Third, defend your decisions to keep parts of the piece "as is," and why you change others, touching on strong uses of criteria noted in your cover letter's thesis.

In writing in this genre, the entertaining writer is a purpose-respecting, rule-valuing member of a community—hopefully a classroom that is one, or, at least, a group that includes people who value academic writing, including you, your professor, me, and many others. The values are textual ones—a good life understood as arguing a position you and your readers find persuasive. To play hard, of course, means to make your argument-based writing as persuasive as it can possibly be. To that end, the rest of this chapter describes an approach to revising an essay by using three new strategies: using higher-order criteria, a peer-authored evaluation, and online editing tools. I will continue to use Meghan's piece—in revised form—as my model. The strategies I describe include individual and collaborative activities.

I first want to reprint part of Meghan's revision, which includes a cover letter describing the changes she made to her paper *and* the first half of the paper. Given that you have access to the complete original, an excerpt is enough to demonstrate the type and quality of her revisions. Where she has used **boldface**, Meghan is explaining revisions she made or why she decided to leave some portion of her work "as is." Where she has highlighted text, Meghan is marking off text that is new to the revised version of the piece. Here is Meghan's work.

---

### BOX 4.2 REVISION COVER LETTER

In my paper, "Is Clifton Park, NY a post-materialistic town?" I chose to explore Bill Bishop's ideas of post-materialism through something in my town that interested me: the music scene. I also used churches, the financial situation, and politics as examples to prove my argument that according to Bishop's definition of post-materialism, Clifton Park is and is not post-materialistic. After getting feedback from three of my peers, they all basically said that I did good work on my paper and could not see anything that had to be improved. However, I do know that my paper still has flaws and is not perfect, so there is always room for improvement.

Overall, I left most of my paragraphs alone because I felt that they sufficiently argued their ideas the thesis proposed with facts and examples to back it up. The paragraphs I did change were mostly to better work on connecting paragraphs to the thesis. In my paragraph describing the political party break down in my town; I added a few sentences clarifying what the paragraph was about and how these statistics can be interpreted to connect to Bishop's theories. Also, in my paragraph describing how Albany and Saratoga are politically different from Clifton Park, I added an example from a local newspaper describing a protest.

Another change that I made was a little reorganization. In my paragraph describing Bishop's ideas, I moved around a few sentences to where they would fit better. I also moved and created a few sentences to the paragraph describing the relationship between my town and two different towns.

The final changes that I made were transitions. I added transitions and sentences to almost every paragraph to clarify my points. In the beginning and end of almost every paragraph there are connections between the paragraph above it and the thesis.

While driving down the streets of the quiet suburban town of Clifton Park, NY, it is hard to believe that during the night, swarms of people flock to the local music venue to listen to bands performing metal, hardcore and punk music. It is also hard to believe that protests are happening just twenty minutes away in bigger towns such as Albany and Saratoga (I did not mention Saratoga in the paragraph talking about neighboring towns, so I fixed this). Clifton Park seems to be undergoing change. During the 1950s and 1960s, there was a cultural shift going on in America. Citizens were becoming more and more polarized in their culture as well as with their politics. Bill Bishop, author of The Big Sort points out that there was dropping church attendance rates, decreasing trust in the government and an increased need for self-expression during this time. Bishop describes the individuals living at this time as "post-materialists." These post-materialists are concerned less about physiological needs and more about self-expression. According to Bishop's description of post-materialistic individuals, Clifton Park could be seen as both materialistic and post-materialistic due to the several different factors. Evidence such as music scene, education, and economy in this town proves that it is post-materialistic. However, church attendance and politics can prove that there are other lifestyles other than post-materialism in the town. (I added more to my thesis to better tie it into the paragraphs and to develop the idea out more)

Bill Bishop bases part of his theory of post-materialism by referring to Abraham Maslow and Ronald Inglehart. (I added this to better explain what will be talked about in the paragraph) Abraham Maslow, a psychologist known for creating the hierarchy of needs theory in 1954, puts physiological needs at the bottom of the hierarchy followed by safety, love, esteem, and finally self-actualization (Maslow). Ronald Inglehart from the University of Michigan created a hypothesis based of Maslow's theory proposing that "People who knew that their basic needs were satisfied would gradually adopt different values from those who live in scarcity." and "those who grew up in abundance would be more concerned with self-expression" (Bishop 2008, 84). Materialists are said to be concerned about economic growth, ability to feed family and military security. Since Bishop defines prosperity as being able to satisfy basic needs, those who did not have to worry about when or how they would get their next meal, would go on to seek other issues. These individuals are more interested in the environment and human rights issues such as gay rights and abortion. Also, they tend to have a higher degree in education. Bishop names these individuals with a need for self-expression as post-materialists and culture creatives. (I felt the need to make it clear that these people are describing post-materialism)

The politics in Clifton Park seem to neither prove nor disprove that Clifton Park is post-materialistic. In Bishop's book, he explains that there is a sorting of neighborhoods and towns into groups that seem to have the same values and political party. However, according to *US Election Atlas*, 50.8% of Saratoga County voted Democratic for Barack Obama in 2008 and 47.45% voted Republican for John McCain. In 2010, 53.18% voted for Democrat Andrew Cuomo and 39.93% voted for Republican Carl Paladino for governor (Leip 2012). Both of these elections are pretty close in terms of the breakdown of Democrats to Republicans. Bishop describes post-materialists as being "cultural creatives" and tending to have a Democratic lifestyle. However, according to this data about Saratoga County, the towns seem to be split almost evenly between Republican and Democrat, which does not support Bishop's idea that the cultural creative post-materialist towns, or "cultural creatives" are predominantly Democratic. (I added this sentence to further clarify that Clifton Park is neither a Democratic nor Republican town, which better ties this paragraph to the thesis and proves that the town's politics does not prove or disprove that it is post-materialistic) Also in Clifton Park, there have not been any large political sit-ins or protests; which is what is expected of post-materialists.

Clifton Park is right in between two famous and completely different towns, Albany and Saratoga Springs. (I moved this from another paragraph into here because it fits better and is used as a transition/topic sentence) Unlike Clifton Park, twenty minutes away in Albany; there are many actions taken that make Albany's residents seem like they trust traditional institutions and the government. Recently, there was a sit in to protest budget cuts to UAlbany, where students walked out of classes to meet in a quad and protest. Through this protest, they expressed their need for change and hopefulness that Andrew Cuomo would deliver. Also, there are many lobbyists in Albany supporting opposing an array of issues, such as the SUNY budget cuts and redistricting. Another example of Albany trusting the government is unions. There are many labor and teachers unions operating out of Albany, including a plumbers union, carpentry union and my dad's union, CWA 1101 (Communications Workers of America). Twenty minutes away in the other direction, is Saratoga Springs. Saratoga is host to all sorts of protests. One of the most recent protests was in March. The protest consisted of teachers and students opposing tax cuts to their school districts. Danielle Sanzone from The Saratogian recalls "Sue Sedon and Kristy Matthews held up a sign stating "Silly, Cuomo, Cuts Aren't for Kids" and a cardboard coffin with "the arts," "sports," "music" in small print and in large print: "You are Killing Us." (The Saratogian). Even a few towns over, Clifton Park is completely different it seems than its neighbors, who seem to trust government institutions. (I added examples of how Saratoga Springs is different from Clifton Park because I had mentioned it in my intro, but not in the paragraph. Also, I feel like giving another example of a town strengthens my argument even further. Also, I like the idea of how these towns can be seen as relying on government action.)

You can see that the cover letter describes the type of changes Meghan made in her revision. She has improved transitions that emphasize each paragraph's main idea and how it reflects the thesis's argument as well as new support. These efforts show she revised to showcase her argument—a good sign it was her heart in the paper. When you look at the revised paper, too, you can see she has done what she said she did in the letter—a move that makes her seem fair and knowledgeable. (Her use of "I" language in the letter has a similar effect. She doesn't seem stuffy. She seems honest, direct, as if she values her subject matter as well as the time any reader might spend with her work.)

As I've explained already, whether you are playing a game or writing-to-entertain, you can use rules to achieve your purposes. I detail three of these now.

### Strategy #1: Use Higher-Order Criteria-Based Questions to Determine Potential Changes.

Not all writing tasks make you think as much or have equal cognitive challenge. That is to say, writing an analysis is going to make you think—make you wrestle with your material—more than is, say, a summary (Newell 2006). I say this to make an analogy: if you do not want to be wasting your time, you want to revise in ways that develop your thinking in the most extensive way. Thomas Reigstad and Donald McAndrew (1984) divide textual qualities into two types: "higher-order concerns" or HOCs and "lower-order concerns" or LOCs. HOCs are the "big" stuff that is most closely related to making your argument persuasive—things such as thesis, organization, and support. LOCs are the "little" stuff—sentence-level errors and MLA style. Even though the "little" stuff, used well or used poorly, does impact how persuasive your writing is, the "big" stuff impacts persuasiveness more because it more directly pertains to your message (i.e., how you arrange your work and the supporting arguments and evidence you use must reflect your point, or you will at least be open to the charge of being "off message"). Working on the "big" stuff—as in the analogy above—also asks you to reflect on your purposes in a deeper way than does, say, deciding to break a long sentence up into two shorter ones. So, if you want to stop wasting your time when writing, focusing on HOCs is a good bet.

A good writing curriculum is going to use as consistent a language as possible for describing effective writing. That is, the same terms (thesis, support, etc.), whenever possible, are going to be used on assignment sheets and rubrics, when a teacher guides students in evaluating a model essay, during teacher-student conferences to describe what a student needs to work on, etc. The idea is that, for a particular section, "support" as a term becomes more and more meaningful as a semester goes on as its members' shared experiences accumulate (they become "the people who know that statistics aren't the only type of evidence out there, but that definitions, analogies, etc. are all options and can be good given the circumstances").

So, your task as a writer is to value the HOCs your class values. One way of doing that is to ask questions of your work that reflect those values. Here is a list of such questions, designed for an assignment using Bishop's *The Big Sort*:

1.  Thesis
    - Does your paper's thesis argue how an event, issue, or the culture of a place, group, or organization in a community supports or challenges Bishop's theory of the "Big Sort" or some part of it? If not, explain why.
2.  Organization
    - Do any topic sentences not capture the full content of the paragraphs they introduce?
    - Do any topic sentences not include a tie to the thesis?
    - Note what's missing or hard for you to find, including the following:
        - Summary of the "Big Sort" that suggests what Bishop's argument is and supports that position with quotations and reflection on them.
        - Use of at least one additional scholarly source.
        - Data from the community being studied and reflection on how these data reflect that community's politics over time and today.
3.  Support:

- Note what's missing or hard for you to find, including the following:
  - Counterarguments where the writer refutes his/her position on whether the sort is/isn't supported in his/her issue, event, or culture.
  - Varied support for the writer's argument, including statistics, examples (could include photos), authoritative testimony, etc.

If you look at Meghan's revision, you'll note her argument—as in most essays—is reflected most clearly and completely in her thesis, which I reprint here: "According to Bishop's description of post-materialistic individuals, Clifton Park could be seen as both materialistic and post-materialistic due to the several different factors. Evidence such as music scene, education, and economy in this town proves that it is post-materialistic. However, church attendance and politics can prove that there are other lifestyles other than post-materialism in the town. (I added more to my thesis to better tie it into the paragraphs and to develop the idea out more)." If you compare it with her earlier one, you'll see a few important changes:

1. She's changed it from one sentence into three.
2. She's included direct reference to counterevidence ("church attendance and politics").

I would argue these changes reflect Meghan's faithfulness to her argument—and a sense that it's her heart in the paper. On the first point: What's more important, saying something that showcases what a paper's all about or making sure everything fits into one sentence? What the paper is all about, of course. On the second point: We get more of the paper's plan *and* additional evidence that her argument is a truly entertaining one—one where she refused to let her prejudices get in the way of careful consideration of her topic. She went for it: She made an argument that changed her view of her town.

These revisions could all have started with Meghan asking herself the question, "Does your paper's thesis argue how an event, issue, or the culture of a place, group, or organization in a community supports or challenges Bishop's theory of the 'Big Sort' or some part of it? If not, explain why." There's a thorny paradox imbedded in this question: the conflict between "supports" and "challenges." So, Meghan might have asked herself, "How well am I representing both 'supporting' and 'challenging' here? Aren't I being more faithful to the topic if I refuse to ignore the 'challenging' part? Yes. Keep going, and get it in there." To do similar work, I suggest responding informally to the criteria-based questions on a separate document; reading what you've written; and asking yourself: "How can I get this stuff integrated into my thesis?" Write it big and bulky at first, directly cutting and pasting your new informal material in at first. You can trim it down later—or, if it's all worth keeping, break it into three sentences. Why? Because your argument has got to be your heart in your paper.

To keep going with the value of asking HOCs-based questions to make argument-enhancing revisions, here are two Meghan might have asked herself that concern organization:

1. Do any topic sentences not capture the full content of the paragraphs they introduce?
2. Do any topic sentences not include a tie to the thesis?

If you look at her revision, you'll see many of her changes have to do with adding material at the start and finish of many paragraphs. The one that stands most out to me is her second paragraph. She saw her original first sentence and how it focused on Abraham Maslow; she read her entire paragraph; she considered what she was supposed to be doing at this point in the paper (it's the "background" section); and she saw a problem: She was introducing Bishop here, so she needed to say so, but she was also talking about Maslow—specifically, how Maslow was a source Bishop had drawn on. To look at the original first sentence to paragraph two another way, by only mentioning Maslow, it had no explicit tie to the thesis itself—which was testing Bishop's theory. The Bishop reference in the thesis makes that tie that, for readers, sends a clear, powerful message: Meghan is not "off message" here in any way. She is making her argument with this paragraph, and with the new transitional material, it's crystal clear.

So, by asking these HOCs-based questions, you can be like Meghan and revise for substance, making argument-enhancing changes to your work that take your ideas seriously and develop those ideas because you care about them and so that your readers might understand what this entire paper was really about, anyway.

### *Strategies #2 and #3: Conduct the Evaluation Task and Use Digital Revision Tools Effectively.*

The last two strategies in this genre section include a task and a tool. The former—an evaluation task—is a HOCs-based argument-enhancer, and the latter can be, too.

*Evaluation Task*

The evaluation task is the result of peer review sessions where students didn't get enough training in what to look for, didn't have enough time in which to make meaningful suggestions, and had been conditioned into thinking that—without a grade—there wasn't much of a reason to care when giving feedback to a peer. The fact is that being a part of the same composition class, knowing the same books, and sharing the same textual values matters a lot—a set of ties that bind, making members of a class committed to doing entertaining writing a community of writers with the background needed to give each other incredibly useful feedback. Wouldn't you want a person who has read one of your sources, knows your genre, and is motivated (intrinsically and extrinsically) to give you quality feedback giving you descriptive feedback on your writing? You would, and to make it worth his/her while, all you would have to do is return the favor. It's a beautiful thing—and a learning, growing community of at least two people at work.

Here is the evaluation task, which I have organized around a particular set of HOCs. Again, if you have different HOCs in use in your class, you should substitute the HOCs I have included with those.

*Evaluation Task*

For this one- to two-page paper, you will (1) summarize in a paragraph and (2) describe the strengths and weaknesses of one classmate's place-based case; then, you will (3) draw on those identified strengths and weaknesses and, making specific recommendations, argue how s/he could improve the paper when revising it.

*Requirements*

You must

1. *Have a thesis that argues how the writer could improve her/his student experience paper by exploiting strengths and addressing weaknesses of the paper in satisfying its criteria.* The criteria you need to consider include varied support, a thesis presenting the writer's position on how Bishop's theory applies and/or does not apply to the community of interest that remains the focus of the entire piece, and organization in the form of transitions and appropriate paragraphing. Least important are mechanics/style and MLA issues.
2. *Present the thesis of and summarize the writer's place-based case in a paragraph.*
3. *In describing the writer's paper, concentrate on at least three criteria that reflect its strengths or weaknesses.*
4. *Quote often from the writer's paper.* These quotes are your evidence.

5. *Tie your examples/supporting points back to your thesis's argument throughout the paper, developing your case for how the writer's paper could be improved.*
6. *Conclude by providing a fair, well-informed set of recommendations for how the writer's paper could be improved.* The goal, here, is not so much to be persuasive but—instead—helpful to the writer in improving her/his paper. Selected, specific recommendations are best.

As you will note from Meghan's cover letter, she did not get feedback she found helping in doing her revision. It is important to me—a sign of an entertaining writer—that Meghan was able to say, "the recommendations you gave me are inconsistent with my purposes." Of course, I'm happy when the evaluation task does work out for a writer. When it does work, it takes advantage of a fact that reflects how most writers develop. Specifically, it is harder for a writer to self-assess than it is for her or him to see what is and is not working in another person's writing. So, the evaluation allows you to step in for a peer where s/he is likely to need you most—and it allows a peer to do the same for you.

Fortunately, Meghan did not stop there. Instead, she did a structured revision of her piece that focused on her thesis and organization, mostly, and added somewhat to her use of support, too. Her focus on HOCs is hard to miss here—and if you do similar work, you'll be doing something that mature writers do and that most student writers do not do, and that is make more than surface changes to a draft. I can promise you this: although writing teachers care about good editing, they understand that HOCs are both harder to address and—if addressed—better reflect a commitment to making a persuasive argument. In a word, HOCs-based revisions are a sign of *character*, heroism on the page.

### Digital Revision Tools

The revision task asks you to make use of a common word processing feature to make your revisions on a computer visible: the "reviewing" function. Most good word processing program have a reviewing function (on Word, it's "Track Changes"; on Google Drive, it's the "Suggesting" (as opposed to the "Editing") setting. With either of these on, you are able to keep track of everything you do to an existing piece of writing—physically putting into another color every section you add or move. Both programs also include a commenting feature, which in the structured revision you can use to explain how you were trying to improve your use of particular HOCs with particular changes you made. If you have "Track Changes" or "Suggesting" on, you can also undo any change; as you know, every adjustment is not an improvement, so this gives you the freedom to compare and contrast versions of your work—and settle on the strongest one in the end.

You will keep the "Reviewing" feature on throughout the entire process of revising your paper, including when you do the "highlighting" and "defending" activities described at the end. In Meghan's case, whereas the evaluating task wasn't useful to her, the revision task was. She focused most of her attention on organization-related revisions, the type answering the organization-related questions included under structured revision strategy #1 would have helped her identify. The cover letter emphasizes this focus—but so do, importantly, the boldfaced annotations themselves. I want to show what Google docs's "suggesting" feature looks like by including a shot of part of Meghan's draft here.

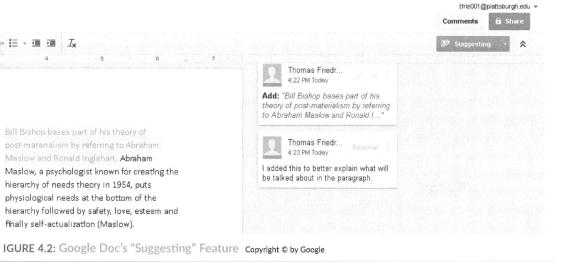

IGURE 4.2: Google Doc's "Suggesting" Feature  Copyright © by Google

This is the start of her revision's second complete paragraph. Where the piece reads, "Abraham Maslow," we see this paragraph's original starting sentence. Because Meghan used another revision strategy—Linda Flower's WIRMI or "What I really mean is … " strategy, where a writer determines a paragraph's main idea and writes a marginal note describing its gist—she saw that her organization could be better here (Meyer and Smith 1987, 96). Specifically, she could see the paragraph was absolutely not about "Abraham Maslow" but Bill Bishop's use of Maslow and another writer's research to make his argument that Americans are choosing to self-segregate into communities of like-minded others. Her revised topic sentence is in green because, on this screen shot, they were made using the "Suggesting" feature.

You can turn this feature on by going to the cluster of buttons ("Comments," "Share," and—below it—"Editing") in the upper-righthand corner of the screen. When you select "Suggesting" from the drop down menu on the "Editing" button, it will become green and be renamed, "Suggesting," which is how it looks in the screen shot. The real power to this revision move was that Meghan could try it out, see what it looked like on the screen, and agree to go with it. It was suspecting and deciding all over again. Using the "Suggesting" feature makes suspecting concrete and, as with the Epicurean life in general, gives you chances to make your writing better that you would otherwise not have had. You can see between the text and the "Suggesting" button a couple of comment boxes. The top one is there because Google creates one whenever you modify text with the "Suggesting" feature on. The second one, though, is a comment box that includes a marginal comment Meghan had originally put in boldface. To create a comment, I recommend selecting the next text you have added and hitting Ctrl-Alt-M, which will highlight the text while creating the equivalent of the second comment box above. In the structured revision, these comment boxes are an opportunity to directly tie revisions to assignment criteria. Because she says that this new topic sentence "better explain[s] what will be talked about," I know she is working on improving her use of the HOC, "organization."

By using the "Suggesting" feature to try out and settle on HOCs based changes in your own piece, you can once more be like Meghan, demonstrating what her work does: we know what she did and that it was a reflection of her effort to internalize the class's idea of what organization means. It's, again, a display of community membership and of character—an identity you can perform, too, by considering the HOCs your class values and using the reviewing feature, highlighting, and annotations to keep track of and publicize your argument-enhancing work.

## Two Assignments with Rubrics

Again, here are two assignment sheets and rubrics designed for possible use with this chapter. The sample papers are responses to these particular tasks. They are printed on separate pages to allow for photocopying.

# PLACE-BASED CASE

For the PBC, you must write an essay arguing how an event, issue, or the culture of a place, group, or organization in a community supports or challenges Bishop's theory of the "Big Sort." You must choose a city in a county to study, your hometown, Plattsburgh, or another community; also, identify its politics using Bishop's election returns maps or searching public records (http://publicrecords.onlinesearches.com/htm) of the area's presidential voting history. There is an undeniable power to using your hometown, given that you have prejudices about it you will be able to draw on and challenge to complete the task; you know a ton about it already, then, and you will be surprised as you learn more. Still, that choice is up to you.

*Requirements*

You must

1. Write an essay that is 1,250–1,500 words in length (five to six double-spaced pages)
2. Satisfy these generic conventions:

   ■ Introduction:
     - Lead that possibly provides an example of the experience of concern to create interest in the case.
     - Thesis that argues how a community example (dis)confirms a social theory.

   ■ Theory: Here you want to introduce at least some part of Bishop's theory that you are going to test against a case. You will want to summarize his argument. You will also want to introduce, define, and provide borrowed or invented examples of categories important to your analysis.

   ■ Background: Here you want to provide some general evidence on the community of interest and possibly the topic. Here public data can be particularly valuable.

   ■ Test Case: Here, you want to draw on varied evidence regarding the topic, the aspect of a community's life you are using to test whether a social theory is or is not validated in this place.
     - Quotations from locals are essential here.
     - A multimodal set of sources is valuable, too, reflecting contemporary experience and suggesting you have done a thorough job.

# PLACE-BASED CASE RUBRIC

| | A | B | C | D | F |
|---|---|---|---|---|---|
| **Thesis** | Focused thesis identifies topic and sophisticated argument, previews essay, possibly acknowledges counterarguments | Identifiable, focused thesis refers to topic, but argument is less sophisticated | General, obvious thesis; argument unclear | General, obvious thesis, if any; lacks discernable argument | No thesis |
| **Support** | Establishes authority through integrating, and interpreting source material, including direct quotations, that support argument | Cites and integrates source material; interpretation tied to main idea of paragraph, mostly; supports argument | May use source well in some sections, but argument feels somewhat lost | Superficial use of predictable, unreliable evidence, possibly not drawn from source at all | No evidence drawn from source |
| **Organization** | Topic sentences introduce paragraphs focused on single ideas connected to thesis. Within and between paragraphs, transitions link and order ideas. | Topic sentences usually but not always connected to thesis. Transitions sometimes missing. Also, overall plan clear. | Topic sentences don't identify main paragraph ideas or connect with thesis. Transitions often missing. Also, multiple or changing plan(s). | Topic sentences and transitions lacking. Is disorganized. | No topic sentences, transitions, or discernable plan. A fragmented work. |
| **Publication Style** | Perfect page format and in-text citations. | Perfect page format. One to two mistakes on in-text citations. Still, citations consistently present. | Some attention to expected page format (title, page numbers, etc., may be missing). Repeated mistakes on in-text citations, but they are present in some form. | Expected page format ignored. Source goes uncited at nearly all points in the paper. | No expected page formatting or in-text citations. |
| **Mechanics** | Free of errors; none or few mechanical errors | Few errors; perhaps some repeated errors but none that make meaning unclear. | Some repeated errors that sometimes make meaning unclear | Weak mechanics | Weak mechanics |

## STRUCTURED REVISION

For this paper, you will revise your PBC so that it is most importantly different and possibly of improved quality. You will do so by selectively considering the comments you received; then, you will focus most of your revisions on your use of higher-order criteria, such as thesis, support, etc.—everything except for MLA style and mechanics. As with the PBC, you must write an essay arguing how an event, issue, or the culture of a place, group, or organization in a community supports or challenges Bishop's theory of the "Big Sort."

When you are finished with this revision, include at the beginning of your revised paper an at fleast 250-word cover letter that describes how you sought to improve your paper by revising to exploit its strengths and address its weaknesses in satisfying its criteria. Before you turn this letter and revised paper in, finally, highlight all changes you made to your revised paper and use the suggesting feature to defend why you kept parts of the piece "as is," and why you changed others, touching on strong uses of criteria noted in your cover letter's thesis.

If you make no (or a few lower order) changes, include no cover letter and do not annotate (put highlights and comments) your paper, you will get an F. If you make a few higher-order changes but richly defend your original text with comments and cover letter that explain how you sought to satisfy higher-order criteria, you will at least get a B. If you make and defend in your comments and letter many higher-order changes but do not improve the overall quality of the piece, you could get an A. If you make and defend many higher-order changes that do improve the overall quality of the piece, you certainly will get an A.

# STRUCTURED REVISION COVER LETTER RUBRIC

| | A | B | C | D | F |
|---|---|---|---|---|---|
| **Thesis** | Presents clear, sophisticated argument for how you sought to improve your PBC by revising to exploit its strengths and address its weaknesses in satisfying its criteria | Identifiable, focused thesis refers to topic, but argument is less sophisticated | General, obvious thesis; argument unclear | General, obvious thesis, if any; lacks discernable argument | No thesis |
| **Support** | Clarifies and develops your argument by including evidence that shows and interpreting how you exploited strengths and addressed weaknesses in specific criteria (with particular attention to use of quotes) | Cites and integrates essay excerpts; interpretation tied to main idea of paragraph, mostly | May use essay well in some sections, but argument feels somewhat lost | Superficial use of predictable, general evidence, possibly not drawn from essay at all | No evidence |
| **Organization** | Topic sentences introduce paragraphs focused on single ideas connected to thesis; transitions within and between paragraphs; intentional organization or plan clear | Topic sentences usually but not always connected to thesis; transitions sometimes missing; generally well-organized | Topic sentences don't identify main paragraph ideas or connect with thesis; transitions often missing; multiple or changing plan(s) | Topic sentences and transitions lacking; disorganized | No topic sentences, transitions, or discernable plan; fragmented |
| **Mechanics** | Free of errors; none or few mechanical errors | Few errors that do not distract | Some, repeated errors that occasionally distract | Weak mechanics | Weak mechanics |

CHAPTER 5

# BEING A NETWORKED USER

Entertaining writing begins with a focused, everyday topic that interests you. In this chapter, that topic is being a networked user of digital tools and texts. You may be a fan or a critic of these objects; personally, I hope that you are a little of both. Regardless, though, you have a personal history of having used computers to foster friendships, to do homework, to play games, to buy and listen to music, and more. In other words, computers are a taken-for-granted part of how you communicate with others. Because of that taken-for-granted status, I use the first part of this chapter to share examples and theories you can use to reflect on the meaning of digital interactions in general and to you as an individual. Second, as in Chapters 3 and 4, to two genres you can use to do entertaining writing on being a networked user: the technological literacy autobiography and the dialectical podcast.

## Digital Tool Use That Makes a Difference: Valuing Freedom, Choosing Turtles

Researchable ideas for writing about yourself as a technology user appear when you focus on *how* you use particular tools. Why? Broadly speaking, these uses can have profound consequences for your own and others' freedom. Let me explain. Digital tools allow you to make and share objects and—because the sharing gives you access to others' creations—to make *different* objects in the future. This means networked digital tools are potential ways out of old thinking, or taste-transforming cheddar-and-bacon cupcakes at the ready. I say "potential ways out" because simply using technology does not guarantee you'll arrive at new conclusions. Digital tools are great copiers. Use these tools repetitively—to consume a diet of the dullest digital donuts available—and your freedom will be the bankable property of a few elite actors, including the U.S. government, Bill Gates, and their ilk. However, use digital tools to challenge your prejudices, and you will tap the interests you democratically share with others to arrive at a more durable form of freedom. The idea is that you have insights to contribute that I would never think of and could benefit from, and vice versa. So, an apparent weakness becomes a strength: you can't do whatever you'd like, but you and I both get to learn and grow.

Let's look at some examples of freedom-enhancing digital tool use. Can anybody do it? It might not seem so. Consider Edward Snowden's exposure of the Patriot Act's mass phone data collection program. The Patriot Act is a post-9/11 law that, in the interest of catching terrorists, legalized "roving wiretaps, searches of business records, and conducting surveillance of 'lone wolves'—individuals suspected of terrorist-related activities not linked to terrorist groups" ("Patriot Act." *Wikipedia*). Now, an interesting thing about Snowden is that he basically was the Patriot Act—a government employee with largely unrivalled access to information on ordinary people—and then decided he couldn't do it anymore. Some call Snowden a traitor, but what interests me most is that he used digital tools to reflect on his prior course of action and, then, used them to change federal laws and data collection practices.

Snowden's case is extraordinary, but I am convinced that his decision to use digital s differently was not. Here is how he describes is decision to become a whistleblower:

> When you're in positions of privileged access like a systems administrator for the sort of intelligence community agencies, you're exposed to a lot more information on a broader scale than the average employee. ... When you see everything, you see

them on a more frequent basis and you recognize that some of these things are actually abuses. … [O]ver time that awareness of wrongdoing sort of builds up and you feel compelled to talk about [it]. And the more you talk about [it], the more you're ignored. … [E]ventually you realize that these things need to be determined by the public and not by somebody who was simply hired by the government. (Rodriguez, 2013)

Snowden no doubt had rare access to government data, but you can see how his tool use gradually led him to a different, democratic conclusion. The switch was slow—a change of positions that strikes me as ordinary, as evidence that prejudice-challenging networked users can arise everywhere.

All this kind of free digital tool use involves is a little bit of learning. Let me give you an example of a very ordinary prejudice-challenging networked user—1992 me—to show you how. I had a personal computer, a Macintosh SE, which my parents had bought me in 1990. To me, that computer—along with the hundreds of networked lab computers around campus—was basically a typewriter strapped onto a portable file cabinet that could also play Tetris. One friend of mine, though, had different ideas on what a computer was for. At the time, I was an RA for a freshman hall, and so was he. I noticed he was spending loads of time in the computer lab, so I asked him why. He said he was sending and receiving email messages from friends in Japan. I felt I understood why he did this—he had grown up there. Paid for by student fees, email also seemed free. At the time, email held no appeal for me. Why sit at a terminal when I could walk across campus to speak with my friends? I did not feel underserved by more popular technologies (phones, sidewalks, etc.). This changed when one of my best friends spent a semester abroad in Rennes, France, during spring 1992. I don't remember what got me started writing emails to my friend, but I know each one I received felt like an unexpected gift—an addition to my day that made me feel connected and global. Soon, I was regularly writing electronic messages in the lab right next to my staff member.

In 1992, writing emails made me a networked user who could communicate at will on a global scale. It was an awesome feeling, and for good reason: As I would later come to see, I was being the kind of networked user I believe the survival of the world is dependent upon: an *informed* user of digital tools. As an informed user of email, I possessed three traits:

1. *Appreciation* for email (I wanted to communicate with my friend and now I could—in a new way that expanded my options, my world.)
2. *Invention* of digital texts and/or tools (I was actually creating something—in this case, messages to my friend.)

3. *Distribution* of digital texts and/or tools (I was sharing perspectives with my friend and becoming knowledgeable about using email.)

I like to spell out these traits, but they can be compressed into the idea of belonging to a "participatory culture" of digital tool users (Lankshear and Knobel 2010, 14). When I participate in a culture of users, I do so because I appreciate the tool (email-as-medium) and—as participant—I use it to invent things (emails I wrote to my friend). Because my use takes place within a culture that gives me thoughts (is an email a letter?), I share mine in return (any Francophiles out there?). I'm not alone in describing and celebrating the importance of the informed user. Axel Bruns calls her/him a "produser," the idea being that there is no absolute division between producers and consumers or users of texts and tools anymore (Lankshear and Knobel 10). There was a time when one party made the product or message, another received it, and ne'er the twain did meet. Hans Magnus Enzenberger argues this division ended with "transistor radio" signals listeners could potentially use to communicate back with the stations that sent them (Wardrip-Fruin and Montfort 2003, 262). Few listeners did, of course, and that's the way the radio stations liked it. Networked computers changed this. Richard Beach et al. (2009) explain this through the idea of the "Web 2.0." On the early Internet, or Web 1.0, some did the talking and others, the listening. By contrast,

> The user of Web 2.0 tools assumes an active role as both a participant in and contributor of information on the Web. ... Rather than simply passively accessing information on websites, in creating and responding to blogs, wikis, podcasts, or chat sites, students are actively constructing and sharing their own knowledge ... [with] immediate and [potentially] worldwide audiences. (6)

In writing transatlantic emails to my friend, the 1992 me was "actively constructing and sharing ... [my] own knowledge" as an appreciating, inventing, and distributing informed user.

The 2019 me is still writing emails, but I've definitely lost something. I'm not excited by my inbox anymore, which suggests that being networked—in and of itself—is no assurance that informed use will follow. There is something undemocratic and unfree about me as an email user today. Email was once a choice. Now, I'm in a very different place, one Sherry Turkle (2011) describes as the experience of being "alone together." Always online, I can choose when and how to reply; I feel powerful. The feeling, though, comes at a price: I don't need to write *now*, so I wait, I fester. It begins to feel it doesn't matter when I reply—or even if I reply at all. As Turkle puts it, "When media are always there, waiting to be wanted, people lose a sense of choosing to communicate" (163).

How did I get here? I would argue I have lost a sense that being a networked user means belonging to a "participatory culture" of invested, creative users. I would argue, too, that this is something that tends to happen to most users when they have been using the same technology for a long time.

So, what does a user do to get out of this place? A new tool is a possibility, but are there tools available that are particularly powerful platforms for informed use? According to Seymour Papert (1993), the answer is yes. Papert calls digital tools that afford users many opportunities for appreciation, invention, and distribution—such as a game like Minecraft or a photo-editor Photoshop—"turtles." Whereas you can almost play Candy Crush in your sleep, a photo loaded into GIMP will not "Photoshop itself" into something else. It will just sit there and present you with thousands of options—much as a blank word processing screen will not write a paper for you. This demand for problem-solving or "debugging" a turtle provides two benefits to users that stand out to me. First, it makes error-making an essential, community-joining experience of using the program. Second, it makes learning hard to avoid and meaningful, as playing turtle involves "get[ting] started on becoming more articulate about one's debugging strategies and more deliberate about improving them" (Papert 1993, 23).

How do you remain a prejudice-challenging, informed networked user? In my view, you will use turtles to solve problems with others who share the same goal. If you stop solving problems—or start hoarding your answers—it's time to move on to a new problem, a new turtle, or both. The answer is: be the kind of person who falls in love with serious tools and other people who love them, too. The answer is: geek out.

I want to spend the rest of the chapter introducing two digital genres you can write in to grow into a more informed networked user: the photo-edited Technological Literacy Autobiography and the Dialectical Podcast. As in previous chapters, I'll present strategies designed to make writing in these genres more meaningful, including some suggestions about using appropriate turtles (GNU Image Manipulation Program (GIMP) (https://www.gimp.org/) and Audacity).

## Genre #1: Photo-Edited Technological Literacy Autobiography

The photo-edited Technological Literacy Autobiography (TLA) is a genre associated with a trailblazing Writing Studies researcher: Cynthia Selfe (2004, 59). It's a type of literacy autobiography, something education majors are often assigned to write. Broadly, all literacy autobiographies have the same goal: to build an awareness of how one learned and was taught, informally or formally, to read, write, or communicate using digital tools and texts. A TLA focuses on that list's last item—on your history of communicating with digital objects such as word processing software, social networking platforms, online video games, and so on. I like TLAs for a couple of reasons. First, a TLA is a welcoming basis for describing and reflecting on your tool use because it asks you to write about your past. Second, a TLA emphasizes support over argument and organization, unlike a lot of academic writing. Third, a TLA is a natural match for doing multimodal writing because our digital tool use histories are multimodal—integrating image, sound, and gesture.

A TLA has some basic generic characteristics:

*Introduction*

- *Lead* that showcases who you are as new media user (consumer and producer)

- *Thesis* that answers this question: How did you develop into a new media user, ideally emphasizing how you are both fan and critic?

*Body*

- *Selective history of digital tool use*, a story that describes your uses of tools that were most important and that provide sufficient evidence for who you are as a new media user

- *Use of literature on new media* to define what you take new media to be and what it means to be an informed producer and consumer; while you will emphasize this at the start or end of this section, you must make connections throughout

- *Relevant, modified images and "visual rhetoric"* (arrangement of text and image on page, typography, and analysis of images (Purdue OWL Visual Rhetoric) reinforce thesis and meaning of events included and conclusions drawn about them

- *Relevant hyperlinks*

- Return to your thesis, rooting your claims in tool use experiences and literature noted in body

Note how much of the paper is in the body; that reflects the importance of support here. If you lack it, you will fail. If you have it, you will sail. Definitions and arguments are notoriously difficult things to write. The good thing is, with a TLA, you can't attempt to write either one of these things cold, out of thin air. No, instead, you'll gather evidence and—as you eliminate redundant parts of your tale, as you find excerpts from new media literature that reflect ideas of appreciation, invention, and distribution or involvement in a "participatory culture" in your digital tool use—you'll begin to arrive at your definition of informed use and of who you are as a new media producer-consumer.

Here is an example of an excerpt from a student's TLA, enough material to demonstrate a TLA's look and feel.

---

### BOX 5.1: TLA

#### NEW MEDIA: NEW ME

The younger generations, of which I belong, may say that we are not exceedingly interconnected with our media outlets. However, we *are* intricately linked with these modern, frivolous—yet quite useful—communication technologies. According to the *Oxford English Dictionary*, new media is used to describe a field of mass communication through digital technologies. After some lengthy reflection I realized that I have, in fact, used new media to create an identity through social media. I have had the privilege and pleasure of connecting with people miles away from me, all from my cellphone. I have gained highly pertinent skills through specialized tools and programs offered online. I have a give-and-take relationship with new media and the best part is ... that I am still learning about myself through these technologies. So I sit down in my comfy chair, log into my computer, and scroll through my new media history.

As a child of the late 1990s and early 2000s, I experienced the dawn of social media platforms such as Neopets online, Webkinz, ClubPenguin, Myyearbook, and Myspace. As I grew older, I joined more unsupervised online communities such as Facebook, Tumblr, and Instagram. My progression from strictly regulated to more loosely regulated sites, allowed me to create a unique social media identity. Similarly, Cory Doctorow's novel, *Little Brother*, presents the character of Marcus, who defines himself by his online communities. So much so, that these communities leak into real life. Harajuku Fun Madness is an online/offline game and subculture that brings gamers on game-related adventures in the real world. Like Marcus, I joined communities such as these. Perhaps not to the extreme of the teambuilding, puzzle-cracking, Harajuku, but I chose to identify with groups of people through online communities. Although Doctorow's image of new media and identity falls more on the expert level, I can definitely relate to Marcus as a character. I consistently communicate with my friends via social media. My proficiency with these websites has grown out my early entrance into online communities.

As a kid I begged my parents to let me use social media, because it was an opportunity for freedom. The creators of these specific online communities built worlds that allowed me to take on the responsibility for a pet or to decorate an entire household. I was acting as an adult in these live stream worlds. My parents were not telling me to feed kittymittens0103 every day; it was up to me to keep these online pets "alive." Looking back, I was more apt to take care of these electronic animals than my real live pets. I gained a sense of duty and care while watching over my online companions. Specifically in regard to Webkinz, I could go to the real-world store and purchase a stuffed animal and then go online to create a life for my new pet. I recall building rooms (a polka dot room, a purple room, a cooking room), designing outfits (yes, they wore clothing), and befriending other Webkinz in hopes of creating a happy life for my animal. I was a member of many other communities similar to this one, all of which brought me to the next phase of my new media development.

With this newfound responsibility, I no longer wanted to hide behind the identity of a white Persian cat; I wanted to convey who I was as a person within a different, more sophisticated, online community. So I launched into the realm of Myspace *Shudders.* ... My identity outside of this website was fragile. My friends and I all matched our worth to our ranking on someone's "Top Friends." Though I gained a sense of responsibility in my earlier online communities, this morphed into a binding obligation to update my status every day, multiple times a day, and perfect each picture that featured any sort of physical blemish. ... I needed to understand how unhealthy this use of new media was for my emotional self. Lankshear and Knobel (2010) support the idea that new media offers a pathway toward identity fulfillment. However, at this point in my life, new media was hampering my true self, rather than facilitating it. Lankshear and Knobel write that "[new media] offer[s] some temporary or provisional sense of normality and existential safety" (13). While I agree that I was seeking refuge online, away from high school life, I felt just as lonely using these social media websites.

**FIGURE 5.1:** Disgust Meme  Photo: Copyright © maria (CC by 2.0) at https://commons.wikimedia.org/wiki/File:Disgust2.jpg. Meme was created with makeameme.org.

... My relationship with new media is tricky. It taught me to be responsible for online companions, it brought me solitude in times of complete adolescent angst, and it opened new doors for discovery as I enter adulthood. But it also provoked a part of myself that I did not like. No matter its use—social media, photo editors, or means of communication—new media is an immanent part of today's culture and we must use it responsibly. So, I speak to members of the younger generations: use it wisely and use it well. I no longer want to be known as a member of the generation who cannot log off their computer or look up from their phone. I want these two worlds, the real and the online, to be interconnected. A cooperation across the real and digital realms.

In Sky's TLA, her thesis on how she developed as a new media user in that phrase: "I want these two worlds. ... A cooperation across the real and digital realms." Coming at the end of her piece, it reads like the intersection of a personal odyssey and new media literature (Doctorow; Lankshear and Knobel) because all of the support necessary to make a strong body is here. First, the personal odyssey emphasizes the idea that she is both fan and critic: her argument that she "wants these two worlds, the real and the online," bridges how she develops from fan of digital community spaces (Neopets, etc.) to a critic of more sophisticated social networking platforms where she learned to deal with the rigid norms of the "heterosexual market" (Eckert and McConnell-Ginet 2003, 26). There would be no odyssey without this conflict, which reflects the DNA of any good story: the elements of "Character + Predicament + Extrication" (Gottschall 2012, 186). You will need a conflict, too, to make your TLA effective. But back to the other elements that make this body work. You'll note Sky focuses only on her use of social networking platforms in her TLA. Using a similar focus on one type of digital tool in your TLA could serve your purposes well, too, allowing you to treat several events in detail instead of feeling forced to breeze through a list of moments. Two ideas for other, similarly focused TLAs include being an online music consumer/producer and being a digital photographer. To return to Sky's piece, though, look at her effective use of visual rhetoric. Her visual rhetoric is at its best with the "When I Look at Old Facebook Posts" meme, which connects beautifully with her complicated history with social networking platforms while also being hilarious. (Also hilarious is "kittymittens0103." I mean, isn't it?). Sky uses diverse yet selective support on her social media tool use history to reveal the argument that she wants "these two worlds" yet "cooperation" across them, and you can do similarly focused work in your TLA.

### Strategies #1 and #2: New Media Experiences (NME) Inventory and Literary and Experiential Themes (LET) Chart.

To help you get started, let me ask you question: How did you develop into a new media user, ideally emphasizing how you are both a fan and critic of digital tools? Your answer to this question will, in a sense, give you the topic for your paper with little effort. Your challenge, then, is to make an evidence-based argument about how you developed—and, most importantly, to showcase that evidence in your body. So, how to get there? Use your body-building—a relatively easy task—to reveal your argument, a much more challenging one.

### NME Inventory

To begin your body-building, I recommend starting off by figuring out what story of digital tool use you are going to want to tell. Whether you already know what type of tool you want to focus on (e.g., social media platforms, photo-editing software, music producing/consuming software, etc.) or not, a great place to start developing your story is an NME inventory. Here is an example:

TABLE 5.1: NME Inventory

| Name a new media tool you have used, beginning with your earliest memories | Describe an experience you have had that you associate with this tool |
| --- | --- |
| Nintendo Entertainment System | I remember this machine, released in 1985, mostly because my parents refused to buy one for me. They thought it would be bad for my brain, cut away at my social interaction, and other arguments you can imagine. |
| Apple IIGS | This was the first PC my parents bought, and it entered our house in 1986. I remember it had Steve Wozniak's (one of Apple's co-founders) signature on it—or at least a version of his signature that he was willing to let be printed on 50,000 computers. |
| Macintosh SE | My own first PC (thanks, Mom and Dad). Again, a community hub, but in this case, in the dorms. |
| Google docs/drive | |
| iPhone | |

This strategy is useful because it lets you forget you're going to have to write a paper for a while and, instead, take up the far easier task of listing the digital tools you remember using. As you begin to fill in the lefthand column's slots, starting with your family's early hardware—its first computer or game system—can be good. So can starting with early programs you used, as Sky did. You are going to want to have both, particularly as hardware becomes less important and the Internet more central to all of our lives as digital tool users. The righthand portion of the table is, of course, useful at beginning to develop moments that might go into a TLA. But the righthand portion of the table is particularly well-suited to revealing themes that might be part of your TLA's argument. Of course, doing an NME inventory does not write a TLA for you, but it's a low-stakes, flexible tool for getting started and beginning to see what you might choose to include in your autobiography.

Now, let's pivot toward the thesis: The above stories suggest ways of limiting the scope of a TLA, but they don't turn directly to its argument, to questions like this:

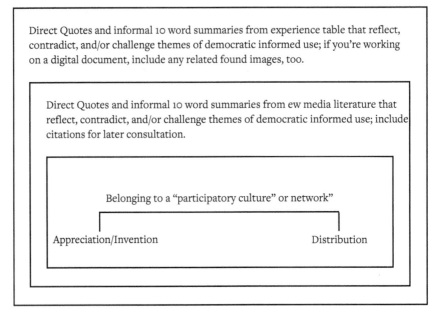

Direct Quotes and informal 10 word summaries from experience table that reflect, contradict, and/or challenge themes of democratic informed use; if you're working on a digital document, include any related found images, too.

Direct Quotes and informal 10 word summaries from ew media literature that reflect, contradict, and/or challenge themes of democratic informed use; include citations for later consultation.

Belonging to a "participatory culture" or network"

Appreciation/Invention                      Distribution

FIGURE 5.2A

1. What are new media?
2. How might an informed user of digital tools and texts be defined?
3. Finally, who *you* are as a new media user?

Answering that last question will involve turning to your stories, but if you ignore the first two questions, they won't tell you what you need. Using a LET chart, though, to guide a strategic reading of new media literature and your NME inventory will, though. My goal is to have you, first, look for examples of and exceptions to these themes in new media literature; then, working on a document or by hand, you should start adding that material to a version of this chart. Draw lines between the words in the center of the chart and similar points raised in what you've read and written. Or, as I do in my example below, just use the lines on the chart to organize what you include. If you find there are new terms you'd like to add to the center of the chart, then add them. If you find my terms are not working for you, you don't have to use them in your TLA, but don't scratch them out; their purpose is to keep you from reducing new media to something less than meaningful, social digital tools and tool use.

Belonging to a **"participatory culture"** (Lankshear & Knobel 14) or network"
- a "produser" (Lankshear & Knobel 10)
- the Xnet (Doctorow)

**Appreciation/Invention**
- Marcus's creation of the Xnet
- VampMob (Doctorow 305)

**Distribution**
- The press conference (Doctorow 235)
- VampMob (Doctorow 305)

FIGURE 5.2B

Now, to the literature. I suggest looking at introductions to edited volumes because they make arguments that their contents belong together in a book. You can test those arguments against the themes I present in the chart below. Some useful introductions include the following:

1.  Colin Lankshear and Michele Knobel's "DIY Media: A Contextual Background and Some Contemporary Themes" (https://narrateannotate.files.wordpress.com/2016/05/lk2008ch1.pdf).
2.  Janet Murray's "Inventing the Medium" (https://monoskop.org/images/4/4c/Wardrip-Fruin_Noah_Montfort_Nick_eds_The_New_Media_Reader.pdf. This is a link, in fact, to an entire anthology of new media texts; you'll find Murray right at the beginning.)
3.  Lev Manovich's "New Media from Borges to HTML" (https://faculty.georgetown.edu/irvinem/theory/manovich-new-media-intro.pdf).

None of these are easy reads, but as Lankshear and Knobel's chapter's title suggests, they present themes you'll be able to use to scrutinize the ones I've placed at the center of the chart. Interested in an idea of what new media are? Look at what Manovich (2013) argues the term means to the "popular press":

> new media are the cultural objects which use digital computer technology for distribution and exhibition. Thus, Internet, Web sites, computer multimedia, computer games, CDROMs and DVD, Virtual Reality, and computer-generated special effects all fall under new media. Other cultural objects which use computing for production and storage but not for

final distribution—television programs, feature films, magazines, books and other paper-based publications, etc.—are not new media.

Now, I'd argue Manovich refers to the "popular press" and "cultural objects" here because this list ignores the role users play creating these objects. Still, this quote helps clarify explicitly what are new media. The other texts help in the same way.

For a more richly developed, accessible and fun treatment of the same themes, I suggest turning to novels on new media. Here are three that would work well:

1. M. T. Anderson's *Feed*
2. Cory Doctorow's *Little Brother*
3. Ernest Cline's *Ready Player One*

You can go a long way toward coming up with a rich definition of new media and an argument for who you are as a user by turning to any of these novels. Paired with one of the edited collections' introductions noted above, you'll be on solid, interesting ground for filling out a LET Chart—and for developing your TLA's body.

### Strategy #3: GNU Image Manipulation Program or GIMP.

This genre asks you to edit images, too, because they are an increasingly essential part of effective writing today. If we can define writing as "effective symbolic expression" (Herrick 2008, 7)—the use of systems of symbols (like letters and characters) to communicate messages—then we can consider other symbol systems types of writing, too. Consider these pictures of my left hand. I am sending different messages with each, particularly the "thumbs up" (approval) and "peace" (welfare) signs. If those gestures are writing, as I take them to be, then images have a place at the table when it comes to doing academic writing—particularly the entertaining writing I am asking you to do in this book in general and the TLA in particular.

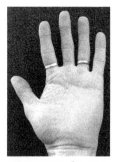

**FIGURE 5.3:** Gestures demonstrating different messages

You'll recall the larger point that the success of the TLA depends on lots of body-building that supports your argument for who you are as a new media user. With respect to images, this raises two points: First, you want to find and modify images that reflect your digital tool and text use history, and second, the edited images you include should all reflect and engagingly, entertainingly draw attention to your argument for who you are as a new media user. I see these points displayed in Sky's model clearly. Every effective piece of entertaining "creative" or "academic" writing has some kind of hook, an example or question or definition that provokes and focuses the reader on what's to come, and Sky's is no exception. When she writes, "So I sit down in my comfy chair, log into my computer, and scroll through my new media history," she places two cropped screenshots—of herself logging in, of a "history" search on her browser—right next to the phrase. In this way, she uses text and image to demonstrate that she has "used new media to create an identity through social media." That, of course, anticipates her thesis, just as it should. But I'd argue that this pairing of text and image also creates a feeling of immediacy, of shared adventure, for the reader. If you tell me you've got a history of using digital tools, I know something I knew before. But if you pair it with images, and your history becomes specific to a particular time and place—I get to go on an argument-testing journey with you. Found, modified images help us go along for the ride with Sky, and you can use them in the same way. Images distill arguments, too, as Sky's Kirsten Wiig meme shows; it reflects the same ideas about social media skepticism she develops in the MySpace paragraph, but she communicates them in a flash. Distaste, regret, a change in Sky's role within a "participatory culture": it's all there, hard evidence that the problem—how do I use an image to make an argument for who I am as a digital tool user?—is challenging and fun to solve.

FIGURE 5.4A: Screenshot of Creative Commons search bar  Copyright © by Creative Commons.

Part of what makes this task challenging is the infinite number of photo-editing choices GIMP offers you. Fortunately, restricting your options can make the challenge of creating an argument-centered, modified image manageable. One way of restricting your options—and not breaking laws—is to start your search by entering the names of (categories of) hardware and software from your NME Inventory into one of the Creative Commons (https://search.creativecommons.org/) search engine's image options, like Flickr (https://www.flickr.com/). Provided you give credit, you can manipulate pretty much any image on Flickr as much as you'd like. If you do an advanced Google Image search (https://www.google.com/advanced_image_search) and use the "usage rights" option to find only images you are "free to use share or modify," you'll be in the same position.

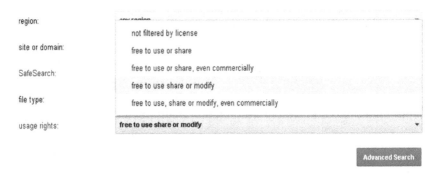

FIGURE 5.4B: Screenshot of Google advanced image search bar and license drop down menu Copyright © by Google.

The liberating power of fewer options becomes clear when you open up GIMP. Once you've downloaded and opened the program you'll see two windows: the GIMP toolbar (with tabs titled "File," "Edit," etc.—that is, your garden variety, MS Word-style options) and toolbox (which I've included here and is, because of its image-specific options, allows you to focus on modifying images in meaningful, argument-centered ways; if you accidentally close it, hitting Ctrl-Alt-B will bring it back). One of the easiest ways to create a meaningful, argument-centered image is to choose a base layer that shows a new media tool or text and then add to that additional layers, lines, or text boxes that allow you to emphasize something about that original image. To do this, you will only need to perform a few steps. You'll use one of the image search tools noted above, and download your image; open GIMP, click on the "File" tab, click on "Open," find your image, and open up in GIMP. Or, you could take a screen shot (hit Ctrl-Alt-Print Scrn), open GIMP, create a New image (it's under "File"), hit Ctrl-V, and use the crop tool (see below) to eliminate what you don't want. As far as modifying found images on GIMP goes, a few tools are all you need:

a. the crop tool ( □ ),
b. the move tool ( ✛ ),
c. the scale tool ( ⛶ ),
d. the text tool ( A ), and
e. the intelligent scissors tool ( ✂ ).

FIGURE 5.5: GIMP tools (a) crop (b) move (c) scale (d) text (e) intelligent scissors tool Copyright © by GNU Image Manipulation Program (GIMP).

Numbers one to three allow you to change size and location; and number four allows you to add a textbox to an image. Number five is more complicated, but what it allows you to do is cut an image out of a larger one. To do this, you left click around the edge of an object—leaving an inch or so between clicks; once you close the loop, left click one more time inside the area you selected so that your loop starts flashing. Hit Ctrl-C, create a new image, then Ctrl-V, and you'll have a cut out you can paste on top of any other image. There is no substitute for experience here. With a little practice, though, you could create something like my "Um, hello?" Macintosh image. You'll recall that way back in 1990, I got my first PC, a Macintosh SE. To emphasize how I didn't see at first but later discovered how that made me a networked user, I placed an image of a cloud and a textbook with the phrase, "Um, hello?" next to the computer's telephone jack. It's an entertaining, modified image I could use in a TLA to argue who I am as a new media consumer/producer.

If you have never used a photo-editor before, you will no doubt find this process painstakingly slow. But it *will* put you in a position to do entertaining writing—to write-to-learn on a topic you value. If you save your work in stages; tap Ctrl-Z to undo the edits you hate; and consult a peer, your teacher, the

FIGURE 5.6: Toolbox Copyright © by GNU Image Manipulation Program (GIMP).

GIMP handbook, or Google to find your way out of problems, you will be able meaningfully modify images for your TLA. To add your final images to your TLA—regardless of medium (Google doc, MS Word, a blog, a website, etc.), export them as .jpg files (an option under GIMP's "File" tab) and import them into your chart or draft.

## Genre #2: Dialectical Podcast

A podcast is a digitally produced and distributed show, and it can do pretty much everything an essay can in terms of allowing you to use language and evidence to make a compelling argument. As I like to tell my students, the only thing you lose is punctuation. And what do you gain? You gain the opportunity to splice actual voices of others into your work (your "quotes"), to layer sounds on top of one another (every show has a theme song), and more. It's a great bargain. Podcasts are undeniably a form of academic writing today, as programs like Melvyn Bragg's *In Our Time* (http://www. bbc.co.uk/programmes/b006qykl) or Robert Harrison's *Entitled Opinions* (http://french-italian.stanford.edu/opinions/) show. Another comprehensive page with links to a range of educational shows (including "Science Friday" and "Gardening in the Zone") and podcast-making advice, *Podcasting in Education* (https://podcasting-in-education.wikispaces.com/home), makes the same point. Although most argue podcasts need to be distributed publicly, I disagree; emailed attachments count in my book, and they give makers a chance to focus on understanding an idea over communicating it with clarity to a listener—on process over product. Of course, there are many different types of shows, and the range of podcasts is the same. One type of podcast genre is the dialectical podcast. So what's a dialectical show? A show you know, but dialectic you may not. A way of understanding dialectic is by looking at how it's different from a similar concept—dialogue. On one hand, dialogue implies possible consensus between opposing viewpoints on a topic. On the other hand, dialectic plays opposing viewpoints off one another, but it asks you to take a side in the end. It's rhetoric in the classical sense: you entertain both perspectives as you go, but in the end, you have a choice to make.

There are many foci a dialectical podcast can have. The list of controversial issues is endless, as this Wikipedia page (https://en.wikipedia.org/wiki/Wikipedia:List_of_controversial_issues) suggests; some resources connect controversies with "pro" and "con" sources you can use, including library databases such as Gale's Opposing Viewpoints (https://www.gale.com/c/opposing-viewpoints-in-context) and handouts like Evergreen Valley College's "Guide to Sources for Current or Controversial Topics (http://www.evc.edu/AcademicAffairs/Documents/Current-Controversial-Topics.pdf)." Given the focus of this chapter on being a networked user of digital tools and texts, I am going to focus on one controversy here: whether or not our use of digital tools and texts makes informed users more or less likely. I call this the "deus ex machina" or "god from the machine" podcast, with a quote from Janet Murray (2003) in mind:

> [t]he promise of the web, not as it is, but as it could be, is like that of the book before it: it will allow us to say more complicated things to more people with greater understanding. The promise is that we will not be crushed by our own knowledge … because we will organize it together in a vast distributed and synchronized effort. We will not be prisoners of [our tools] … , we will be … the gods of our own machines. (11)

Considering this quote, the question—"how probable is an informed new media user today?"—becomes more concrete, a choice between the statements, "we as tool users are likely to 'crush' ourselves" and "we are fit to be 'the gods of our own machines.'"

Although I've always assigned this genre as a collaborative project, it need not be. An advantage of making it collaborative is that group members get to pool their resources as readers and writers.

Like different types of shows, podcasts vary in their contents. As Jason van Orden (http://www.howtopodcasttutorial.com/05-choosing-your-podcast-format.htm) writes, a "Tech News" podcast may have—among other "segments"—"Announcements," "Top 10 Tech News Headlines with Commentary," and more; a "review show (movies, food, etc.)" may have a "First Review," "Second Review," and "Interview."

A dialectical podcast must contain the following:

*Introduction*

- Provide lead that defines and/or describes your controversy and possibly your position on it while appealing to audience for (an episode of) a recognizable kind of show.
- Establish who host(s), narrator, and so on is/are.

*Body*

- Descriptively present the core event(s) you use to define and/or describe the opposing viewpoints on your controversy (summarizing, analyzing, and citing appropriate sources) and establish which position you consider persuasive.

- Include and meaningfully order multiple sections (rounds, interviews, scenes, commercials, Q&A, etc.) so that your position begins to emerge as the most persuasive.

- Rebut counterarguments, so that you don't arbitrarily choose a winner but show how position is logically, ethically, and/or pathetically stronger or truer than the other.

### Conclusion

- Present your thesis (position on controversy with evidence/ reasons drawn from the show).

- Address implications of show, considering the thesis (describe important, interesting points raised; notable conflicts; significance for audience; imaginary future episodes that may somehow respond to your episode; etc.).

Clearly, whatever position on your controversy your group decides upon will be the organizing focus of your podcast, but if you're wondering what that position is going to be, don't. In fact, at the start, you should avoid any attempt to nail down what kind of show you're going to make; your whole focus needs to be on closely listening to what your sources say about your controversy. For this reason, if you're going to be choosing your own controversy, now is the time to identify it and find your sources (see "Opposing Viewpoints," etc., above). Personally, I give students the controversy and the sources, too: Seymour Papert's *Mindstorms* and Sherry Turkle's *Alone Together*, which take opposing views on the probability of creating informed users of digital tools today. My rationale? This is not a research paper. It's an exercise in closely reading and clearly writing about opposing perspectives on a topic.

So much for direct transmissions of wisdom. Solving the problem of creating a dialectical podcast requires focused practice, strategies that can help you reach your goal. I will get to useful writing-to-learn tools soon, but for now, I want to turn to a student model that illustrates how a popular genre can guide and ground analysis: an episode of the fictional game show, *Network It Out*. At the same time, because it's easy to miss out on a lot of nuance in the audio, read this transcribed excerpt from the program as you listen to the podcast.

## NETWORK IT OUT

[*Upbeat, jazzy theme song plays, fading out after a few seconds.*]

Dix Mercury (*Human co-host, in upbeat, booming tone*): "Welcome to another galactic episode of Network it out. I'm Dix Mercury, and this is my fully charged co-host Mr. 00110101101020100128.001 MK 2.0."

Mr. 001 (*Robot co-host, in metallic, balanced tone, speaks the following numbers, mimicking code*): "010."

Dix: "I'm just as excited, Mr. 001. This time around our 10 contestants faced our hardest challenge yet: To be or not to be with technology! On the last season of Network It Out, our contestants barely survived the three grueling days of reading archaic, cellulose-backed books. What kind of chaos are we cooking up for our new contestants this time, Mr. 001?"

Mr. 001: "010010100110."

Dix: "That's right. This season we're separating our ten contestants into two groups of five, allowing only one of these groups to keep their technological assets."

Audience (*gasping*): "No!"

Dix: "A journey no one wants to endure. To be without their phone for a whole weekend! Maybe our team without their technology, the Floppy Discs, will develop an appreciation for what they have. But who can tell with the opposing team, the TurtleBots. They may be crushed under the pressure that their phones demand of them, the constant attention, the ignorance to others, the retina-searing LED screen. We'll be finding out all of these answers and more in tonight's episode of Network It Out! Here we have our team with technology, team TurtleBot. Team TurtleBot consists of Elle, Botchko, Magnus, Lunaria, and Retu. All are around the age of twenty-two and have never met each other before. Why don't we see how they're getting along?"

Lunaria: "326-875-6523."

Magnus: "326-745-2110."

Dix: "Well, I guess there's no need for name introductions; it seems that all of the contestants exchanged phone numbers and are now proceeding to text each other. How about that for some team bonding, huh, 001?"

Mr. 001: "1001011."

Dix: "You can say that again. Looks to me like Team TurtleBot is off to a good start. We can just see their smiles, although it's hard to tell because their heads are bent so low over their cell phones. I can only imagine the chiropractor bill they get a month. You don't have to worry about those problems do you, Mr. 001?

Mr. 001: "Beep."

Dix: "Look at that Mr. 001, Botchko just frowned in Retu's direction. That can only mean drama in the near future. Are the TurtleBots not so cordial with each other as we first thought? Maybe the delicious buffet set out by our crew will help our contestants bond?

Mr. 001: "0101."

Dix: "Indeed that steak does look juicy. But our contestants are ignoring the mouth-watering aroma. They're still tapping away on their phones. How can our TurtleBots turn down a free meal? If they're not going to eat it, I sure will. ... But wait, Lunaria seems to notice the fresh dinner. She picks her head up and . .

Lunaria: "Food?"

Dix: "She's noticed. She's heading over to the dinner—confused, while licking her lips.

Lunaria: "WTH LOL."

Dix: "How interesting, Lunaria is showing signs of web-speak. This is a coming of age language still in its developmental phases but clearly taking an importance in our TurtleBots."

Mr. 001: "110."

Dix: "And yes the others are ignoring her—you are right—but she doesn't seem to mind as she's feasting away. So much for my dinner! We'll just split the bill at space station, huh, Mr. 001."

Mr. 001: "Beep 1001110."

Dix: "Why don't we check back in with our TurtleBots later and see how they're getting along after spending the whole night together? Stay with us, folks, after hearing a word from our sponsors."

Commercial (*Electronic background music opens, fading to a level where it plays throughout the advertisement. Spokesperson with booming voice begins*): Buy buy buy buy sell sell sell! Come on down to Carthax Boro's House of Tinkering and buy buy buy buy sell sell sell! We guarantee you'll find a price for all of your selling needs. We also guarantee the lowest price on all those astro trinkets you picked up on the way here. Don't be shy! Fly on in to Carthax Boro's House of Tinkering!"

Dix: "And we're back with *Network It Out*. Before the break we checked in on the Turtle Bots to see how they were doing. Now let's see how our other team is settling in. Team Floppy Disc have just entered their respective team headquarters and begun introductions. Their room stripped of all signs of technology—reduced to its natural state—is no more than a prehistoric cave.

Audience: (*All gasp in horror. Then, one woman screams.*)

The signs that this is a show are everywhere. It's a type of show (game) and has a theme song that recalls *The Price is Right*; it has hosts (Dix Mercury and Mr. 001), a gasping audience (thanks, free-to-use prerecorded sounds), and sponsors ("Carthax Boro's House of Tinkering"). The fact that the writers (and co-stars), Annie and Ole, wrote up a word-for-word treatment of the show in advance also reinforces Network It Out's high-stakes, winner-take-all game showness. Still, all of this would be of little value were it not taking a side on a controversy. Annie and Ole's controversy is clear early on in the show, though, where Dix says,

This time around our ten contestants faced our hardest challenge yet: To be or not to be with technology! ... Maybe our team without their technology, the Floppy Discs, will develop an appreciation for what they have. But who can tell with the opposing team, the TurtleBots. They may be crushed under the pressure

> that their phones demand of them, the constant attention, the ignorance to others, the retina-searing LED screen.

Beyond identifying the controversy itself—does our use of digital tools and texts makes informed users more or less likely?—Annie and Ole also take a position on it. In their treatment, they argue, "Technology will further the divide between human interaction and (or devaluing relationships) replace our ability to value others." So, they're taking the "less likely" stance, but of course, they need support to make it persuasively. The core evidence comes from invented examples: the actions of the two teams, one of which (the "TurtleBots") is seen in the excerpt. Teammates who introduce themselves with a clinical exchange of phone numbers and who forego dining together for a nosh? These examples reinforce the podcast's position on the controversy nicely. What is less evident, however, is how Annie and Ole are responding to sources their sources—Papert's *Mindstorms* and Turkle's *Alone Together*. Their lack of direct quotations from these sources is a problem. Still, it's an effective dialectic podcast—a convincing, controversy-focused show with a clear position—with only one strike against it: little direct use of their main sources. To you I say: they did well; now, you do better. To that end, here are some more strategies.

### Strategies #1 and #2: Read-to-Record and Use the Podcast Treatment to Arrive at a Position on the Controversy.

One barrier to making a dialectical podcast is learning to use Audacity (http://audacity.sourceforge.net/download/window), a free sound editing program. A way to meaningfully get past that obstruction is using your skill in reading-to-write (Chapter 2)—where you go on the hunt for a text's argument by informally taking notes on its contents—to make daily informal recordings to sources on your controversy. I ask my students to post these as .mp3 files to Tumblr.com pages, which strangers can't find unless you give them your address, are easy to share with your peers and teacher, and make uploading .mp3 files pretty simple.

But to get to the most important point: If you don't know your sources' perspectives on your controversy, you won't have anything to say about them in your podcast. So, when you read-to-record, you only concern yourself with closely following what your sources are arguing and how those arguments relate to the controversy.

*Read-to-record*

At this point, then, your use of technology should be focused on a few steps: (1) making a Tumblr page for your class, (2) making a recording on Audacity, (3) exporting that recording as an .mp3 file, and (4) uploading it to your Tumblr page. As an aside, there is no shortage of podcast-making resources out there; these include Audacity tutorials (http://manual.audacityteam. org/man/tutorials.html) as well as more general sites (see sites from Apple (https://itunespartner.apple.com/en/podcasts/overview) and How Stuff Works (https://computer.howstuffworks.com/internet/basics/how-to-pod-cast.htm). In general, I'd say if one source does not work, try another. I give you my list of steps because—as with GIMP—I believe that limiting options can be liberating, so here are what you need to learn how to do to get started creating your dialectical podcast. First, you can create a page for your daily recordings at Tumblr.com; once you are in, the page you'll want

to work on is the dashboard—visible above—as this page has the purple headphones icon ("audio") you'll click on when you have your .mp3 file ready for uploading. If you want to check out your Tumblr page, you can get there by tapping on the torso icon to the left of the rainbow colored buttons; provided you stay logged in, you can click on the Tumblr dashboard address (https://www.tumblr.com/dash-board), and it will take you right back to that page. Second, download Audacity. You will note it's de-signed to look like a tape recorder, which helps. Making a recording is as simple as hitting the red "record" button and having a microphone.

FIGURE 5.7: Tumblr Toolbar Copyright © by Tumblr, Inc.

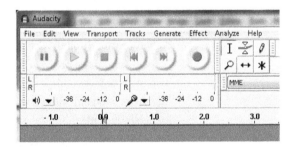

FIGURE 5.8: Audacity Toolbar Copyright © by Audacity.

Third, export your recording. No doubt this is the hardest step of the four. If you are recording on a PC, you will need to export your file using the Lame encoder (visit http://lame. buanzo.org/, and download the file named, "Lame_v3.99.3_for_Windows. exe"). It takes a little practice; I'd say the main thing is knowing where your sound files are being placed by the program.

If you have a smartphone, the microphone problem disappears. With an Android device, you can download Audacity Portable (https://portableapps. com/apps/music_video/audacity_portable). As with people who create their individual recordings using the PC version, you will need to convert your files to mp3s before you post them. If you have an iPhone, you can use the "Voice Memos" app to record .m4a files and send them to yourselves as email attachments. Then, you can download Audacity onto a PC. Your next step is to prepare Audacity to accept .m4a files by downloading the Lame MP3 and FFmpeg encoders onto your PC. An easy way to download and install these encoders is to watch this tutorial (http://www.youtube.com/ watch?v=20SXcPwkq34). I listened to this once without stopping and then a second time, stopping as I performed the acts she describes. Once you have Audacity downloaded on your computer, you can go to the aforementioned website to find these encoders (http://lame.buanzo.org/). The mp3 conversion file is this one: "Lame_v3.99.3_for_Windows.exe"; here, you'll find the m4a conversion file: "FFmpeg_v0.6.2_for_Audacity_on_Windows.exe." (You can't click on these ".exe" file addresses to download them; you must use the "lame1.buanzo.com/ar" one.) Once you have installed these encoders, you can open your m4a file on your PC using Audacity, export the file as an mp3, and upload it to Tumblr. To upload your .mp3 file to your Tumblr page, click on your dashboard's purple headphones, find your .mp3 file, confirm that you have the right to post it (which you do, as it's your work), and you'll be set.

You will learn to perform these tasks by making informal reading responses to sources on your controversy. You can use this general approach:

> When you are through with the assigned selection, record a one-
> to two-minute response. ... Before you start recording, identify
> two to three ideas and/or brief quotations expressed in the read-
> ing. Attach to your Tumblr site. Share your site with your group
> members and me.

Not concerning yourself with what your podcast will look like in the end, you will read-to-record to identify the selection's argument and how it relates to the controversy. As for the argument, you are in familiar territory; it's a matter of speculating about what a selection's thesis appears to be and confirming it as you go (Chapter 2). To discover its relationship to the controversy, you can use a table of possible themes for each source (Chapter 3), first identifying themes that appear to reflect the "essence" of your phenomenon from the assignment sheet—and, then, looking for examples of those themes and/or replacement/additional themes:

**TABLE 5.2:** Table of Possible Themes

|  | Theme 1 | Theme 2 | Theme 3 | Theme 4 | Theme 5 |
|---|---|---|---|---|---|
| **Selection 1** |  |  |  |  |  |
| **Selection 2** |  |  |  |  |  |

A different approach to discovering your argument involves responding to specific reading prompts. For the informed user probability podcast, here is a reading prompt for Papert (1993, xvii–54):

> When you are through with the assigned selection, record a one-to two-minute response to the following question: *What conditions for informed use do we live in?* Specifically, how does Papert argue people may harness the "holding power" (27) of computers to strengthen teaching and learning? How is the turtle an "object to think with" (7) or "carrier of cultural 'germs'" (9) that "concretizes (and personalizes) the formal" (21)? What barriers to this outcome are there (the "QWERTY phenomenon" (32), "mathophobia" (42), etc.), and how may they be overcome? You do NOT need to respond to all of these questions; respond to the one(s) you connect best with. Before you start recording, identify two to three ideas and/or brief quotations expressed in the reading. Attach to your Tumblr site. Share your site with your group members and me.

I suggest writing down notes on your "two to three ideas" (twenty-five to thirty words) before you hit "record," as it will allow you to be more source-centered (to select quotations, provide page numbers, etc.). If you are creating an informed user probability podcast, here are prompts for other sections from Papert (1993) and Turkle (2011):

**Papert (55–119):** Read and spend five to ten minutes playing turtle (http://logo.twentygototen.org/); when you are through, record a one- to two-minute response to the following question: What kinds of learners and teachers does doing "turtle geometry" create? Informed use may involve invention and distribution, or creating and sharing texts, but those acts must always be rooted in a sense of appreciation or pleasure. How does "syntonic" (63, 97) turtle play where learners "debug" (61) a program's subprocedures (111) reflect this appreciation? Draw on your own experience of playing turtle here, too, if you like. What kind of teacher does playing turtle create (115)?

**Turkle (1–52):** When you are through with the assigned selection, record a one- to two-minute response to this question: What conditions for informed use do we live in? For Turkle, how are our relationships with sociable computers and in networked life simplifying our relationships so that we are left "together and alone" (11)?

Turkle (53–102): When you are through with the assigned selection, record a one- to two-minute response to this question: What kinds of people are our conditions saturated with sociable computers creating? Turkle argues our pragmatic embrace of sociable robots has led us to reduce what relationship means (55) and confine ourselves to a closed world (66). How do the child and adult users of sociable robots she describes reflect and/or complicate this argument?

**Turkle (151–170, 211–228, 279–296):** When you are through with the assigned selection, record a one- to two-minute response to this prompt: What conditions and people have we created through our use of tools that constantly network us? That is, how is being "always on" another way we promote machines and demote ourselves (168)? Consider these people: "Multi-lifing" Pete (160), underperforming multitaskers (163)), Diane the "Maximizing Machine" (163, 165, 172), Rashi the *Second Life* "master builder" (215), *Quake and Civilization* playing Adam who has only "bots" for companions (219), and Turkle's graduate student who proposes "technology as prosthesis" (290). If you like, you may also respond to this last question: What strategies for cultivating informed use does Turkle describe, and do you think Papert would take issue with any of them?

Guided by such prompts, your informal recordings will get you familiar with making recordings using Audacity and how your sources address your controversy as individual texts.

*Using the podcast treatment to arrive at*
*your position on the controversy*

Now, onto the podcast treatment. Writing a treatment—a document that will begin as a note-taking space on your daily recordings and become, possibly, a word-for-word treatment of your podcast's recorded language—will ask you to not only test your initial impressions against others' but also to (1) evaluate how your sources address common themes and (2) decide on a position on the controversy. I have my students make the podcast treatment within a single Google document they add to and revise as they progress through the daily readings toward creating the final composition. Here is a link to a complete word-for-word podcast treatment (https://docs.google. com/document/d/1-7tbDro-u-N5RnuQyxlly-2ag78P-W6jnXs0J96CMhs/

edit). To reflect on your own and peer recordings, use this prompt:

> Represent two to three main points on a google document (may include (1) quotations from assigned sources or group members' informal recordings, (2) important themes, (3) memorable examples of new media producers-consumers, or (4) similarities or differences between your own experiences with and perceptions of new media and views represented in the assigned readings or your group members' informal recordings). Keep adding to this document as you respond to each class meeting's readings.

For Annie and Ole, this practice helped them develop these notes on Papert and Turkle:

- Turkle—Argues that technology is distancing humanity and its bonds; Line between humanity and technology is blurring (CYBORGS):

  1. Using robots for selfish needs: confidante, companion, therapist.

  2. Undermines humanity's capacity for interaction with others.

- Papert—Argues for technology as an educational advancement:

  1. Computer programs integrated into the classroom.

  2. Teachers/professors aware that technology and the utilizing of it through practice may create an enthusiastic informed producer.

  3. Students can relate material in a personal way— rewarded/successful in their efforts to solve problems through a program (debugging).

What I see are (1) working theses of selections from Turkle and Papert as well as (2) memorable/important examples and moments in these sources that reflect those arguments. Side by side, how these sources address the informed user probability controversy for them becomes clearer: it has something to do with "humanity and its bonds" with others and objects. As with the informal recordings, more and less independent approaches can work. As for the more independent approach, a table of possible themes will work here, too. The following box is an example.

| | Theme 1 | Theme 2 | Theme 3 | Theme 4 | Theme 5 |
|---|---|---|---|---|---|
| **Source 1** | | | | | |
| **Source 2** | | | | | |

The major difference is that, instead of testing and finding examples of themes by reading across the assignment sheet and an individual source, you should be reading across all of your sources at this point. For a more directive approach, specific questions on how your sources take similar and different positions on themes associated with your controversy can work. Here are some on Papert and Turkle concerning the informed user probability controversy:

1. To what extent is Turkle's call for people to "put … [technology] in its place" a form of debugging?

2. Turkle and Papert have different views on how our vulnerabilities affect us in our tool use. For Turkle, they hurt us as we fill in the blanks for our sociable robots—telling only the triumphalist narrative. For Papert, our vulnerabilities make us need and allow us to play with the computer as an object to think with. Have your vulnerabilities made it possible for you to learn to create new types of objects using digital tools? To what extent are Turkle and Papert just describing different types of tools?

3. Agree or disagree: Is there a proliferation of tools that make few complex problem-solving demands?

4. Is the computer an object to think with or a companion? What's the difference between the kind of dialogue I have with a tool when I am trying to make something and the kind of dialogue I have with a person?

Whichever approach you use, a core fruit of this analysis should be a working thesis identifying the controversy and your position on it. Annie and Ole wrote the following one in their treatment:

**Thesis!:** Technology will further the divide between human interaction and (or devaluing relationships) replace our ability to value others.

- Informed users because they depend on their tools, which shows their appreciation (comfortable); [still, this use arguably keeps] us … saying "my taste is good enough," not furthering [our] interests.

- Our machines will "crush us"—we will not rule them but they will rule us because of our dependency and ignorance toward others.

The idea of "humanity and its bonds" has developed here into a position on the controversy. Appreciation—a thing fundamental to informed use, as it means the user is intrinsically motivated to use a tool—is also a potential pathway to getting stuck in a "feedback loop," to diminished relationships. Like Annie and Ole, you can use informal recording and reflective writing in your podcast treatment document to arrive at a statement of your position on your controversy.

### Strategies # 3 and 4: Turn Your Podcast Treatment into the Basis for a Show and Use Audacity to Create It

#### Turn your podcast treatment into the basis for a show

Having a "recording-ready" podcast treatment means scripting at least parts of your show; dialogue quality varies, certainly, but it begins with asking questions like this: What would this character sound like? Is he closer to Abraham Lincoln ("Four Score and Seven Years Ago ... ") or Drew Carey ("Audience, don't say a word! You'll cost him/her the prizes if you do. So be quiet. Whenever you're ready, go!")? When Annie and Ole asked themselves this question about how Dix Mercury should sound, they went with the latter. Now, writing dialogue can take a lot of practice. If you have that concern, let me say this: Your task, again, is not to attract an audience. Rather, it is to use a recognizable type of show to express your position on a controversy, which you already know. Still concerned? Imitating a model can carry you pretty far—and that does not just include imitating a particular character but a whole show. You can imitate a show—gaining insights about characters, plot, setting, and so on, for free—by demanding that your podcast be either an imitation of a particular show or, more loosely, a version of a kind of show. To do this, I provide you with this paragraph:

> You must decide what kind of show this will be and make use of its conventions. Will it be a talk show? *Judge Judy* (Turkle and Papert were once married)? A game show? A debate? A PBS Educational special? A press conference introducing the next iPhone? What will your theme song be? What commercials will your show have? Who will be your characters, including hosts, narrators, or guests be? (You can "be" yourself if it suits you.) You will want to script many parts of your show; this will save you time when you are doing your final editing.

Responding to these questions can help you flesh out your show; speaking with someone else (a peer, teacher, fan of a show you are imitating, etc.) as you answer them will help, too. Still, deciding on the type of show you are going to make—as van Orden's segment lists show—will provide you with answers on characters, segments, etc. for free. Let me list two types of resources you may want to consult:

> Lists of show types: Apple's iTunes, Wikipedia's category page for radio programs (https://en.wikipedia.org/wiki/Category:Radio_programs), Apple's Podcast Connect categories (https://help.apple.com/itc/podcasts_connect/#/itc9267a2f12), and the Podcast Awards (https://www.podcastawards.com/; this last source includes lists of winning shows by category dating back to 2005, including links to the shows).

> Lists of and resources on finding show transcripts: NYU's page on Radio Broadcasts and Transcripts (https://guides.nyu.edu/c.php?g=276657&p=1845378), LexisNexis (to get transcripts in this database, use the instructions for finding transcripts on this document (http://www.lexisnexis.com/pdf/academic/nexis-uni/Search-FAQ.pdf)), and this page on finding NPR program transcripts (https://www.npr.org/sections/ombudsman/2009/08/free_transcripts_now_available.html).

How might these resources help you? The value of looking at a list of show types is that it may help you stumble upon an idea—and, potentially, get ideas for free on characters, segments, and so on. Once you've got your show type nailed down, listening to (or watching) a program can further help you flesh out your program—particularly if you consider your program as a parody of that original. Cut back to Annie and Ole: What does Drew Carey say and do as a game show host that makes him create excitement in the contestants? Does he ever seem offensive? His predecessor, Bob Barker, certainly was. What makes your source show itself? This can be a time for more phenomenological analysis—for looking for themes, catchphrases, and more. What could you copy, or modify—just enough—to remind listeners you are responding to that show? It's a form of tribute, surely, to something that attracts or arrests you. Whether fan or hater, parodying another show is a potential goldmine for segment—and dialogue—development. On the dialogue point, because slowing a show down can help you see nuance, I list the transcript resources above. They may help you catch those catchphrases. Or not. To move on, here is a suggestion: open up your podcast treatment document, and write down your type of show and/or the show you intend to parody. It's time to answer some questions. To convert my paragraph above to questions you can respond to on your document,

1.  Why/how might making a [type of show/parody of a particular show] allow you to showcase your position?
2.  Who might your characters be, and how might their actions or motives reflect your position?
3.  What kind of theme song would a show that deals with your controversy have?
4.  What kind of sponsor might be interested in a show like yours?
5.  Every show tells a story. A story on a baseball game is pitched (sorry) to a particular audience; it is designed to highlight heroics, the signature moments that made "all of the difference" in the outcome, the moment in the season that it took place, the fortunes of a particular team during a particular year. What story might your show tell to showcase your controversy and position on it? (For Annie and Ole, the title, *Network It Out*, comes to mind. How could they showcase how digital tools might be making informed users less probable today? There had to be sides. There had to be a conflict. What about teams that couldn't work together? Yes.)
6.  What other segments might help you disclose your position?

As you answer these questions, you will begin populating your treatment with show-based content. Don't delete the source-based notes you've put there, either (at least not until you are far into getting your dialogue down). You may want to begin by naming what segments you think might allow you to make your argument persuasively—and then fleshing them out. You may want to begin by making a commercial. You may want to begin by doing your opening credits. There are many starting points, and the important thing is to be intentional. Suspect and decide. Plan your show.

*Use Audacity to create your show*

With a more- or less-developed plan in hand, you will be ready to once again turn to Audacity, which—like GIMP—is a turtle if there ever was one. It presents you with infinite options for recording and remixing sound, which means there is room for you—regardless if you are a novice or veteran podcaster—to do meaningful work when you hit "Record." With the less experienced in mind, I want to highlight a few features you can use to create a show. Audacity creates, as you already know, files with the .aux extension, and keeping your draft file an .aux document up until the very end (.mp3 file exporting time) will grant you maximum flexibility in modifying it.

To say a little more about maximum flexibility, working on a PC is particularly useful at this phase, as you can use a mouse to make the most nuanced changes as well as import supporting sound files (applause tracks, direct quotes, etc.). The features you are likely to want to use including the following tools:

a.  the selection tool ( $\boxed{\text{I}}$ ),
b.  the envelope tool ( $\boxed{\text{⤸}}$ ), and
c.  the time shift tool ( $\boxed{\leftrightarrow}$ )

FIGURE 5.9: Audacity tools (a) selection (b) envelope (c) timeshift Copyright © by Audacity.

With the selection tool, you will be able to select a moment in time on a track of your sound file. That is mostly useful for playing your work-in-progress so you can use the time shift tool to drag particular tracks to play when you want them to. The envelope tool allows you to adjust the volume at which a certain track will play. By using these three features, you can—as the screenshot displays—have a theme song open your show and fade out to allow the program to begin. Let me explain the few moves I made. I hit "Record," and began reading; that is the top horizontal bar with blue markings in it. I saved that file and closed it. Then, I opened Audacity again, hit "Record," and sang the opening line from the chorus of Bob Dylan's "Lay Lady Lay." (I could have, under "File," clicked on "Import" to add another recording as my theme song.) After saving the Dylan file, I opened the "Reading" file, too. Then, all I had to do was tap on the Dylan file's horizontal bar with blue markings, hit select all (Ctrl-A), hit copy (Ctrl-C), and paste "Lay" into the "Reading" file, for which it became the second, lower horizontal bar. By tapping on the envelope tool, I reduced the sound of "Lay" as you can see. Finally, I tapped on the "Reading" bar and—using the "Time Shift" tool—dragged it to the right, so my theme song would come first. Opening sequence complete. Now, as with GIMP, there is no substitute for practice, and you will spend time getting things right. That's part of the fun, though.

One advantage of recording myself singing is that I could include it without violating a copyright law; I'd have been in even better shape had I recorded an original song, but I'm going to power through. Still, it raises a point: you want to use sound files it is legal to use, ones that—like Flickr images—can be included in your work. To that end, I want to share a few sites where you can find free sounds to finish this chapter:

1.  freesound.org

2. creativecommons.org/audio
3. jamendo.com/en (royalty free music)
4. podsafeaudio.com
5. audiofarm.org
6. freemusicarchive.org
7. ccmixter.org
8. beatpick.com
9. simuze.nl

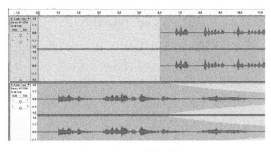

FIGURE 5.10: Audacity Sound File Tracker

It is important that you only use those that allow derivative works. And you can, in a final display that you are—of course—an informed networked user.

## Two Assignments with Rubrics

Here are two more assignment sheets and rubrics designed for possible use with this chapter. The sample papers are responses to these particular tasks. They are printed on separate pages to allow for photocopying.

## TECHNOLOGICAL LITERACY AUTOBIOGRAPHY

For this 1,800–2,400 word paper (six to eight pages), you will respond to this question: How did I develop into a new media producer and consumer? Use Lankshear and Knobel, Murray and/or Wreden to define what you take new media to be and what it means to be an informed producer and consumer; you may do this defining work near the beginning of your paper, but given that this is a story of your development, you may want to integrate your own lived events and insights drawn from these sources to build your definitions, perhaps only disclosing them in the end. You will not only be assessed based on the quality of the text you produce, but also on your use and manipulation of relevant images and your use of hypertext to reference relevant and cited sources (in particular, images you include, fair use of which often involves including hypertext links to your sources' location on the internet).

# TECHNOLOGICAL LITERACY AUTOBIOGRAPHY RUBRIC

Key: 1 = Not working  2 = Needs substantial revision  3 = Adequate  4 = Strong!  5 = Excellent

| | | | | | |
|---|---|---|---|---|---|
| The qualities of narrative as a genre are displayed (uses dialogue, precise detail, vivid verbs; is told from a particular point of view; has conflict) | NA | 1 | 2 | 3 | 4 | 5 |
| **Tone** is "interesting and compelling" to the target audience (Selfe 2004, 104), appropriate to your purpose, and makes you come across as reliable) | NA | 1 | 2 | 3 | 4 | 5 |
| Demonstrates good use of **visual rhetoric.** | NA | 1 | 2 | 3 | 4 | 5 |

By visual rhetoric, I mean "the interplay of context,purpose, and audience perception in understanding and interpreting how visuals are meaningful"(Alexander and Barber 2005, 184).

This includes the following features:
- Arrangement of elements on a page (it is clear and consistent and doesn't conflict with theme of autobiography; creates "striking paths for the eye" that are consistent, unique, readable; has a readable color)
- Use of typography/formatting (font makes you seem reliable; headline and body text emphasize important information such as key terms and concepts, are readable, etc.)
- Analysis of existing images and visuals (highlights main points/supports autobiography, presents information in a visually appealing way (Purdue))

| | | | | | |
|---|---|---|---|---|---|
| Audience-targeted **lead** | NA | 1 | 2 | 3 | 4 | 5 |
| Responds to **question**, "How did I develop into a new media producer and consumer? | NA | 1 | 2 | 3 | 4 | 5 |
| Uses Doctorow, Lankshear and Knobel, Murray and/or Manovich to define what you take new media to be and what it means to be an informed producer and consumer | NA | 1 | 2 | 3 | 4 | 5 |

| | | | | | | |
|---|---|---|---|---|---|---|
| **Unity** is displayed (the work is a single thought) | NA | 1 | 2 | 3 | 4 | 5 |
| Paragraph- and sentence-level **coherence** rovided; clear, consistent organization; deliberate development for a purpose evidenced, etc.) | NA | 1 | 2 | 3 | 4 | 5 |
| **Support** (includes "enough evidence and reasoning to allow your readers to judge if your analysis has been adequate" (Stoll quoted in Alexander and Barber 2005, 200); presents information in effective way, adds appropriate visual elements and hypertext) | NA | 1 | 2 | 3 | 4 | 5 |
| **Visually attractive and appealing** (uses and manipulates images "to highlight certain issues or draw attention to important information" (Alexander and Barber 200); redesigns text in terms of color, layout, etc. (Selfe 104)) | NA | 1 | 2 | 3 | 4 | 5 |
| **Creativity** (unity, coherence, support) | NA | 1 | 2 | 3 | 4 | 5 |
| Audience-directed **wrap-up** | NA | 1 | 2 | 3 | 4 | 5 |
| **Mechanics/style** issues | NA | 1 | 2 | 3 | 4 | 5 |
| **Publication style**, including citations; fair use of Creative Commons material | NA | 1 | 2 | 3 | 4 | 5 |

# THE DEUS EX MACHINA SHOW:

# A DIALECTICAL POCAST

> "*Deus ex Machina is* Latin for 'a god from a machine.' It describes the practice of some Greek playwrightsto end a drama with a god who was lowered to the stage by a mechanical apparatus and, by his judgment and commands, solved the problems of the human characters." (Abrams 1999)

> "The promise of the web, not as it is, but as it could be, is like that of the book before it: it will allow us to say more complicated things to more people with greater understanding. The promise is that we will not be crushed by our own knowledge … because we will organize it together in a vast distributed and synchronized effort. We will not be prisoners of [our tools] … , we will be … the gods of our own machines." (Murray 2003)

In this podcast you should create using Audacity (http://audacity.source-forge.net/download/windows), I want you to answer a question: How probable is an informed new media user today? In other words, *are we as tool users likely to "crush" ourselves, or are we fit to be "the gods of our own machines"?* If we say informed users are unlikely, then, we may say our tool use is likely to "crush" us. If we say informed users are likely, we are making the case for ourselves as "the gods of our own machines."

This collaboratively written and produced, twenty- to thirty-minute show will consist of three parts. First, you should present a definition of what you take an informed user to be, turning to your autobiographies as your evidence. Second, you should draw on Papert and Turkle to answer this question: How probable is an informed new media producer-consumer today? These authors present (somewhat) opposing answers to this question. Papert (1993) argues computers can be "transitional objects" that make formal subject matters concrete, even for resistant learners. Turkle (2011) is less optimistic. Regardless of what side you choose, do not ignore counterarguments. Third, you may conclude by describing projects for becoming a more informed user that appeal to your group members.

You must decide what kind of show this will be and make use of its conventions. Will it be a talk show? *Judge Judy* (Turkle and Papert were once married)? A game show? A debate? A PBS Educational special? A press conference introducing the next iPhone? What will your theme song be? What commercials will your show have? Who will be your hosts or guests (Turkle and Papert can visit them; you can "be yourselves" in the show; etc.)? You will want to script many parts of your show; this will save you time when you are doing your final editing.

One of your group members should submit your podcast to me as an mp3 in a gmail attachment on the due date.

As you complete daily reading sections in preparation for the podcast, you will also post informal, individual audio responses saved as mp3 files to a Tumblr.com site. Here is my site (http://tomfriedrich0.tumblr.com/). I will give you prompts to respond to; you need not respond to all of the questions but, rather, to those that capture your interest most.

You will be graded on the following tasks:

1. Completing all daily, individual blog recordings (30% of total grade).
2. Regularly and thoughtfully contributing to in-class group doc, shared with one another and the teacher as Google doc (20%; this should be shared with the teacher).
3. Your collaborative podcast (45%; this, as well as "draft" recordings, should be saved to one group member's Tumblr site).
4. Your individual assessment of the podcast's quality (5%; this should be shared with the teacher as a Google document). The review should be about 250 words in length, and in it you should answer two questions: First, how does your podcast successfully argue one of the following: we as tool users are likely to "crush" ourselves, or we are fit to be "the gods of our own machines"? Second, how does that success reflect your contributions to the work (both in terms of the process of creating it and the work itself)? Your support, in the form of brief quotations and summaries, should be drawn in a balanced way from your podcast and your individual recordings.

# THE DEUS EX MACHINA SHOW: RUBRIC

Key: 1 = Not working  2 = Needs substantial revision  3 = Adequate  4 = Strong!  5 = Excellent

## Group Project

| | 1 | 2 | 3 | 4 | 5 |
|---|---|---|---|---|---|
| Podcast length, due date, process (all Tumblr posts, collaborative doc, and podcast), citation demand met, suggesting rigorous dedication throughout | 1 | 2 | 3 | 4 | 5 |
| **Titles & subtitles:** "Use of clearly defined titles or use of what are called ID3 tags to display titles that are consistent with the content of ... [the] podcast" (Beach et al. 2009, 141) | 1 | 2 | 3 | 4 | 5 |
| **Generic Conventions:** While attracting interest, introduction tells listeners what to expect from the presentation, introduces argument for what the probability of being a informed new media producer and consumer is today while possibly previewing the podcast; a definition of being an informed new media producer and consumer is provided, with support from your group members' TLAs and TLA sources; in the largest part of the podcast, use Papert and Turkle to defend your position on how probable an informed user is today; and conclude by describing projects for becoming a more informed user that appeal to any of your group members. | 1 | 2 | 3 | 4 | 5 |
| **Support:** Establishes authority through integrating and source material, including direct quotations, that support argument | 1 | 2 | 3 | 4 | 5 |
| **Tone and sound:** "Effective voice enunciation, sound production, and editing as well as use of music or sound effects to create the sense of a show" and "[u]se of voice and language that conveys interest in a topic or subject" (Beach et al., 141–142) | 1 | 2 | 3 | 4 | 5 |
| **Coherence:** "Effective use of well-organized time to focus on the topic or subject in some depth without excessive extraneous talk that consumes extra time"(Beach et al., 141); transitions foreground argument and other main ideas | 1 | 2 | 3 | 4 | 5 |

| Collaboration: Everyone worked well together, sharing decisions and responsibilities (including creating and completing all blog entries that identify and provide evidence of important themes), motivating the group to do its best. | 1 | 2 | 3 | 4 | 5 |
|---|---|---|---|---|---|

## Individual Contributions (enter number in blank)

| | |
|---|---|
| I completed five blog entries that identify and provide evidence of important themes | 0 (least) … . … . … … 5 (all) |
| I richly engaged in in-class collaborative responses/plans | not at all … . … . … . . exceeded expectations |

**Short answer**: Based on the scores you have given yourself, what grade do you think you should receive for this project? Please ground your judgment in examples drawn from your performance on rubric criteria.

# BIBLIOGRAPHY

## Preface

Bourdain, Anthony. "Quebec." *Parts Unknown*, CNN, 2013.

Greenblatt, Stephen. *The Swerve: How the World Became Modern*. New York: Norton, 2012.

## Introduction

Greene, Stuart. "Mining Texts in Reading to Write." National Center for the Study of Writing, 1991. https://www.nwp.org/cs/public/download/nwp_file/52/OP29.pdf?x-r=pcfile_d.

Dillard, Annie. *The Writing Life*. New York: Harper, 2013.

## Chapter 1

Aristotle. "Rhetoric." In *Readings from Classical Rhetoric*, edited by Patricia Matsen, Philip Rollinson, and Marion Sousa, 117–160. Carbondale: Southern Illinois University Press, 1990.

Barthes, Roland. *The Pleasure of the Text*. Translated by Richard Miller. New York: Hill and Wang, 1975.

Boisvert, Raymond. John Dewey: Rethinking Our Time. Albany: State University of New York Press, 1998.

Britton, James, ed. *The Development of Writing Abilities*, 11–18. New York: Macmillan, 1975.

Darnton, Robert. *The Great Cat Massacre*. New York: Random House, 1985.

Davis, Natalie Zemon. *The Return of Martin Guerre*. Cambridge, MA: Harvard University Press, 1983.

Dewey, John. *Art as Experience*. New York: Perigree, 1934.

Dewey, John. *Democracy and Education*. New York: Macmillan, 1916.

Eagleton, Terry. *Literary Theory: An Introduction*. Minneapolis: University of Minnesota Press, 1983.

"Entertain." *Oxford English Dictionary*. 2016.

Gottschall, John. *The Storytelling Animal*. Boston: Houghton Mifflin Harcourt, 2012.

Hacker, Diana, and Nancy Sommers. *A Pocket Style Manual*. 7th ed. Boston: Bedford Press, 2015.

Hillocks, George. *Research on Written Composition*. Urbana: National Council of Teachers of English, 1986.

Kennedy, George. *Classical Rhetoric and Its Christian and Secular Tradition from Ancient to Modern Times*. Chapel Hill: University of North Carolina Press, 1999.

Lucretius, *On the Nature of Things*. Translated by William Ellery Leonard, Project Gutenberg, 2008. Project Gutenberg. http://www.gutenberg.org/files/785/785-h/785-h.htm.

Merleau-Ponty, Maurice. *Phenomenology of Perception*. Translated by Donald Landes. London: Routledge, 2002.

Murphy, James, and Richard Kutula. "The Sophists and Rhetorical Consciousness." In A *Synoptic History of Classical Rhetoric*, edited by James Murphy and Richard Kutula. 3rd ed. Mahwah: Hermagoras, 2003.

Newkirk, Thomas. *The Performance of Self in Student Writing*. Portsmouth: Heinemann, 1997.

Papert, Seymour. Mindstorms. 2nd ed. New York: Basic Books, 1993.

Plato. "Gorgias." In *Readings from Classical Rhetoric*, edited by Patricia Matsen, Philip Rollinson, and Marion Sousa, 59–74. Carbondale: Southern Illinois University Press, 1990.

Plato. "Phaedrus." In *Readings from Classical Rhetoric*, edited by Patricia Matsen, Philip Rollinson, and Marion Sousa, 75–95. Carbondale: Southern Illinois University Press, 1990.

Pollan, Michael. *In Defense of Food: An Eater's Manifesto*. New York: Penguin, 2008.

Robinson, Andrew. *Writing and Script: A Very Short Introduction*. Oxford: Oxford University Press, 2009.

Quintilian. "From *Institutes* of Oratory." In *The Rhetorical Tradition: Readings from Classical Times to the Present*, edited by Patricia Bizzell and Bruce Herzberg. Boston: Bedford Press, 1990.

"White Cheddar Corn Puffs." *Fearless Flyer*, Trader Joe's, 2017. http://www.traderjoes.com/fearless-flyer/article/1694.

Winterowd, Ross. *A Teacher's Introduction to Composition in the Rhetorical Tradition*. Urbana: National Council of Teachers of English, 1994.

## Chapter 2

Bakhtin, Mikhail. *The Dialogic Imagination: Four Essays*. Translated by Caryl Emerson and Michael Holquist. Austin: University of Texas Press, 1983.

Bakhtin, Mikhail. *Rabelais and His World*. Translated by Helene Iswolsky. Bloomington: Indiana University Press, 2009.

Behrens, Laurence, and Leonard Rosen. *What It Takes: Academic Writing in College*. San Francisco: Pearson, 2012.

Bishop, Bill. *The Big Sort: Why the Clustering of Like-Minded America Is Tearing Us Apart*. Boston: Mariner, 2009.

Carr, Nicholas. *The Shallows: What the Internet Is Doing to Our Brains*. New York: Norton, 2011.

Fish, Stanley. *Is There a Text in This Class? Cambridge*, MA: Harvard University Press, 1982.

Friedrich, Tom. "A 'Shared Repertoire' of Choices: Using Phenomenology to Study Writing Tutor Identity," *Learning Assistance Review* 19, no. 1 (2014): 53-67.

Gee, James Paul. *Social Linguistics and Literacies: Ideology in Discourses*. 2nd ed. London: Routledge, 1996.

Hjortshoj, Keith. *The Transition to College Writing*. 2nd ed. Boston: Bedford Press, 2010.

Rosenblatt, Louise. *The Reader, the Text, the Poem: The Transactional Theory of the Literary Work*. Carbondale: Southern Illinois University Press, 1994.

Steinbeck, John. *Of Mice and Men*. New York: Penguin, 1993.

Van Manen, Max. *Researching Lived Experience: Human Science for an Action Sensitive Pedagogy*. Albany: State University of New York Press, 1990.

Wilson, Lisa. *Ye Heart of a Man: The Domestic Life of Men in Colonial New England*. New Haven, CT: Yale University Press, 1999.

## Chapter 3

Anderson, Debra. *College Culture, Student Success*. San Francisco: Pearson, 2008.

Burton, Gideon. *Silva Rhetoricae (The Forest of Rhetoric)*. Provo, UT: Brigham Young University, 2018, rhetoric.byu.edu.

Dince, Rebecca. "Could Your Facebook Profile Throw a Wrench in Your Future?" In *College Culture, Student Success,* 44–48. San Francisco: Pearson, 2008.

Friedrich, Tom. "A 'Shared Repertoire' of Choices: Using Phenomenology to Study Writing Tutor Identity," *Learning Assistance Review* 19, no. 1 (2014): 53-67.

Hardt, Michael, and Antonio Negri. *Multitude: War and Democracy in the Age of Empire*. New York: Penguin, 2009.

Harrison, Harry. *1001 Things Every College Student Needs to Know (Like Buying Your Books before Exams Start)*. Nashville, TN: Thomas Nelson, 2008.

Herrick, James. *The History and Theory of Rhetoric: An Introduction*. 4th ed. San Francisco: Pearson, 2008.

Graham, Paul. "Good and Bad Procrastination." In *College Culture, Student Success*, 86–90. San Francisco: Pearson, 2008.

Lanham, Richard. A *Handlist of Rhetorical Terms*. 2nd ed. Berkeley: University of California Press, 2013.

*Lead, Innovate, Transform*. NASPA Annual Conference. Baltimore, MD. March 15–19, 2014. https://www.naspa.org/constituent-groups/posts/2014-naspa-annual-conference-the-site-is-live.

Moustakas, Clark. *Phenomenological Research Methods*. Thousand Oaks, CA: Sage, 1995.

Oliphant, Thomas. "Abandoned but Not Alone." In College Culture, Student Success, 25–27. San Francisco: Pearson, 2008.

Orr, David. *Ecological Literacy: Education and the Transition to a Postmodern World*. Albany: State University of New York Press, 1992.

Papert, Seymour. *Mindstorms: Children, Computers, and Powerful Ideas*. 2nd ed. New York: Basic Books, 1994.

"Pnyx." *Wikipedia*. https://en.wikipedia.org/wiki/Pnyx.

Renn, Kristen, and Robert Reason. *College Students in the United States: Characteristics, Experiences, and Outcomes*. San Francisco: Jossey-Bass, 2013.

Rosenblatt, Louise. *The Reader, the Text, the Poem: The Transactional Theory of the Literary Work*. Carbondale: Southern Illinois University Press, 1994.

Sink, Mindy. "Drinking Deaths Draw Attention to Old Campus Problem." In *College Culture, Student Success*, 49–51. San Francisco: Pearson, 2008.

State University of New York, Plattsburgh. *SUNY Plattsburgh*, 2018. https://web.plattsburgh.edu/.

Tesich, Steve. "Focusing on Friends." In *College Culture, Student Success*, 40–43. San Francisco: Pearson, 2008.

Van Manen, Max. *Researching Lived Experience: Human Science for an Action Sensitive Pedagogy*. Albany: State University of New York Press, 1990.

## Chapter 4

Bishop, Bill. *The Big Sort*. Boston: Mariner, 2008.

"Capital Region High School Graduation Rates 2009." *All Over Albany*, March 10, 2010. http://alloveralbany.com/archive/2010/03/10/capital-region-high-school-graduation-rates-2009.

*City-Data.com*, Advameg, 2018, www.city-data.com/.

"Clifton Park." *City-Data.com*, April 18, 2011. http://www.city-data.com/city/Clifton-Park-New-York.html.

Dewey, John. *Experience and Education*. New York: Collier, 1963.

Lee, Stephanie. "Students Cut Class in Protest." *Albany Times-Union*. January 28, 2011, A3.

Leip, David. *Dave Leip's Atlas of U.S. Presidential Elections*, 2012, uselectionatlas.org/.

Meyer, Emily, and Louise Z. Smith. *The Practical Tutor*. Oxford: Oxford University Press, 1987.

Murray, Charles. *Coming Apart: The State of White America*, 1960–2010. New York: Crown Forum, 2013.

Newell, George. "Writing to Learn." In *Handbook of Writing Research*, by Charles A. MacArthur et al., 235–247. New York: Guilford Press, 2006.

"Picks of the week—April 14–20." *Albany Times-Union*.

Putnam, Robert. *Bowling Alone: The Collapse and Revival of American Community*. New York: Simon & Schuster, 2007.

Reding, Nick. *Methland: The Death and Life of an American Small Town*. London: Bloomsbury, 2010.

Riegstad, Thomas, and Donald McAndrew. *Training Tutors for Writing Conferences*. Urbana: National Council of Teachers of English, 1984.

Shea, Mike. "Bill Bishop." *Texas Monthly*, May 2008. https://www.texasmonthly.com/articles/bill-bishop/.

Thandeka. *Learning to Be White*. New York: Continuum, 1999.

Van Maanen, John. *Tales of the Field: On Writing Ethnography*. 2nd ed. Chicago: University of Chicago Press, 2011.

Woodard, Colin. *American Nations: A History of the Eleven Rival Regional Cultures of North America*. New York: Penguin, 2012.

## Chapter 5

Alexander, Jonathan, and Margaret Barber. *Argument Now*. San Francisco: Pearson, 2005.

Anderson, M. T. Feed. Somerville, MA: Candlewick, 2004.

Beach, Richard, et al. *Teaching Writing Using Blogs, Wikis, and Other Digital Tools*. Boston: Christopher-Gordon, 2009.

Cline, Ernest. *Ready Player One*. Portland, OR: Broadway, 2012.

Doctorow, Cory. *Little Brother*. New York: TOR, 2008.

Eckert, Penelope, and Sally McConnell-Ginet. *Language and Gender*. Cambridge: Cambridge University Press, 2003.

Herrick, James. *The History and Theory of Rhetoric: An Introduction*. 4th ed. San Francisco: Pearson, 2008.

"Glocalization." *Wikipedia*. https://en.wikipedia.org/wiki/Glocalization.

Gottschall, John. *The Storytelling Animal*. Boston: Houghton Mifflin Harcourt, 2012.

Knobel, Michelle, and Colin Lankshear. *DIY Media*. New York: Peter Lang, 2010.

Lankshear, Colin, and Michelle Knobel. "DIY Media: A Contextual Background and Some Contemporary Themes." In *DIY Media*. New York: Peter Lang, 2010.

Levit, Alice. "Locavore Blue Collar Bistro Opens in Plattsburgh," *Seven Days*, June 4, 2014. https://www.sevendaysvt.com/vermont/locavore-blue-collar-bistro-opens-in-plattsburgh/Content?oid=2376273.

NBC5 "Artists Create New Mural in Downtown Plattsburgh," Burlington, VT. http://organizations.plattsburgh.edu/museum/winkel2.htm.

Manovich, Lev. "New Media from Borges to HTML." In *The New Media Reader*, edited by Noah Wardrip-Fruin and Nick Montfort, 13–25. Cambridge, MA: MIT University Press, 2003. https://faculty.georgetown.edu/irvinem/theory/manovich-new-media-intro.pdf.

Murray, Janet. "Inventing the Medium." In *The New Media Reader,* edited by Noah Wardrip-Fruin and Nick Montfort, 3–11. Cambridge, MA: MIT University Press, 2003.

Papert, Seymour. *Mindstorms.* 2nd ed. New York: Basic Books, 1993.

"Patriot Act." *Wikipedia.* https://en.wikipedia.org/wiki/Patriot_Act.

Rodriguez, Gabriel. "Edward Snowden Interview Transcript FULL TEXT: Read the Guardian's Entire Interview with the Man Who Leaked PRISM." *Mic,* June 9, 2013. https://mic.com/articles/47355/edward-snowden-interview-transcript-full-text-read-the-guardian-s-entire-interview-with-the-man-who-leaked-prism#.OnP4z5Ua5

Selfe, Cynthia. "Students Who Teach Us: A Case Study of a New Media Text Designer." In Writing New Media: Theory and Applications for Expanding the Teaching of Composition, edited by Wysocki, Anne et al., 43–66. Logan: Utah State University Press, 2004.

Turkle, Sherry. *Alone Together.* New York: Basic Books, 2011.

"Visual Rhetoric: Overview." *The Purdue OWL Family of Sites.* The Writing Lab and OWL at Purdue and Purdue University. https://owl.english.purdue.edu/owl/resource/691/01/.

Wardrip-Fruin, Noah, and Nick Montfort. *The New Media Reader.* Cambridge, MA: MIT University Press, 2003.

Printed in the USA
CPSIA information can be obtained
at www.ICGtesting.com
LVHW080546220823
755870LV00001B/21

9 781516 545537